Witchcraft, Superstition & Ghostly Magic

By Daniel Cohen

GROSSET & DUNLAP
Publishers • New York

Originally titled *Superstition*

ISBN: 0-448-11787-8

Copyright © 1971 by Creative Educational Society, Inc.
All rights reserved under International and Pan-American
Copyright Conventions.
Published simultaneously in Canada.
Printed in the United States of America.

contents

Editor's Note

WHAT THE DAISY

REALLY TELLS US

Once the daisy was thought to have great healing powers. It was used to treat such different ailments as mental illness, toothache, rheumatism, and headache. Although the daisy is rarely taken today as a medicine, a remembrance of magic still clings to this pretty flower.

A daisy is supposed to predict the future by answering Yes or No to a question. The questioner pulls off the first petal for Yes, the second petal for No, and so on, until the final petal provides the answer.

The daisy game is a mild superstition that usually is not taken too seriously. Yet it contains this powerful clue to understanding many other superstitions: People who are superstitious often turn over the responsibility of solving a problem to somebody or something else. They may seek answers from a daisy, the stars, or a fortune teller. But they tend to avoid looking into themselves.

While reading this book, you will find many other reasons why people are superstitious. Ignorance and fear are part of the story — as well as courage, curiosity, and hope. Superstitions reveal practically all of humanity's weaknesses and strengths. Perhaps that is why superstitions are so fascinating — even the innocent daisy game can tell us something significant about the way we think and act.

Gene Liberty

Chapter 1

WHAT WILL TOMORROW BRING?

The next time you ride an elevator in a tall building, see if there is a 13th floor. Some buildings have one, but others do not. From the 12th floor, they skip right to the 14th. What happened to the 13th floor? It is there, of course, but it is called 14. In this and similar situations, the number 13 is frequently avoided. The "Devil's dozen" — an old name for 13 — is supposed to bring bad luck.

There is nothing lucky or unlucky about any number. The belief that a number can bring good or bad luck is a superstition held by a surprisingly large number of people. A *superstition* is a belief or practice that does not rely on fact but is usually based on fear of the unknown or on ignorance. Most superstitions are supposed to make something good happen or prevent misfortune.

The 13th guest

The 13th day of the month, particularly if it is a Friday, is regarded as unlucky by superstitious people. Many of us joke about Friday the 13th. But others are cautious about their activities on that day for fear that an accident or other disaster may occur. Some superstitious people also consider it unlucky for a group of 13 to eat dinner together. One of them, according to the superstition, will die within a year.

We do not know how the number 13 got its bad reputation. "Unlucky 13" may have started with the Vikings or other Norsemen. They told the story of a great banquet for 12 guests — all of them gods. The evil god Loki, angry at not being invited, sneaked into the banquet. Now there were 13 guests. One of the gods at the banquet was killed, and since that time — the story goes — the number 13 has been considered unlucky.

Some think the belief started with Christianity. At the Last Supper, there were 13 — Jesus Christ and the 12 apostles. The Last Supper was followed by Christ's crucifixion so that, again, the number 13 was identified with

NUMBER 13 AT THE TABLE
Kaspar, a black wooden cat, is assigned the 13th place when a party of 13 dines at London's Savoy Hotel. The guest who would have been number 13 takes the 14th place.

The hotel follows this practice partly in good humor and partly because some people feel uneasy about the unlucky 13 superstition.

Kaspar himself has not suffered by being number 13. True, he has been catnapped several times. But he always has been safely returned.

5

"OF COURSE THERE ISN'T ANY 13th STORY. THAT'S BAD LUCK."

DEFIANCE OF SUPERSTITION . . . OR IS IT?

Members of anti-superstition clubs amuse themselves by defying bad luck. For example, it is considered unlucky to:

- Walk under a ladder.
- Open an umbrella indoors.
- Cross a knife and fork.
- Spill salt.

Some say that the need to challenge bad luck is itself a superstition. What do you think?

a dreadful event. It is believed that Christ was crucified on a Friday. This explains why Friday is regarded by some superstitious people as unlucky. For example, Friday is supposed to be a bad day to start a new job, to begin a voyage, to cut one's nails, or to get married.

Not so unlucky

It is hard to imagine why 13 is considered unlucky in the United States, a country created by the union of 13 colonies. The first flag had 13 stars and 13 stripes, and today's flag still has 13 stripes.

Look at the two sides of the Great Seal of the United States pictured on the back of a dollar bill. One side has a pyramid with 13 rows of bricks. On the other side is an eagle with 13 stars above its head. The eagle grasps a bundle of 13 arrows in one claw, an olive branch with 13 leaves in the other. If you look closely, you will see that the branch bears olives — 13 of them.

Some people like to defy the belief in "unlucky 13." The Anti-Superstition Society used to meet regularly every Friday the 13th. Once they even gathered in a funeral home and sat around an open coffin with 13 candles on it. The club had 13 vice presidents. To honor a distinguished member, the society gave him a watch with all the hours on it marked "13." All the members of this society were successful men who did not suffer by defying "unlucky 13."

The shield of superstition

We have said that superstitions are usually based on fear of the unknown or on ignorance. Why *usually?* People are not superstitious only because they are fearful or uninformed. Other conditions help to create superstitions. We will examine these conditions, which often are not what they seem to be. Our purpose, in this book, is to explore superstitions, learn how they happen, and understand why they continue to exist.

First, let us look at one simple superstition of everyday life. In this example and in others that follow, we will see how superstitions serve as a shield — for protection against forces that are as imaginary as a ghost or as real as an earthquake.

You have probably heard someone, talking about a good event that may soon happen, stop and say, "knock wood." More than likely, he will even look around for something wooden to knock on. This superstition dates all the way back to the time when men believed the air was filled with evil spirits. If they discussed a good thing, they rapped loudly on wood. Otherwise, the spirits might hear them and snatch the good thing away.

KEEP YOUR FINGERS CROSSED
And, supposedly, a wish will be granted. An ancient belief states that the wish will be trapped where the lines meet at the center of a cross. It cannot escape until it comes true.

Your own image

"Breaking a mirror brings 7 years' bad luck," goes the old superstition. Of course, it is dangerous to break anything made of glass because you may cut your hand. But there are no superstitious beliefs attached to breaking a drinking glass or a light bulb. The mirror is special because you can see your own image in it.

The mirror belief began thousands of years ago, when man thought that his image (picture, sculpture, or reflection) was part of him. He believed, too, that what happened to his image would happen to him.

UNABLE TO RETURN
Why does a broken mirror supposedly bring bad luck? According to one superstitious explanation, the soul is contained in the mirror. If the mirror is broken, the soul cannot return to the body.

7

LOVE OF SELF — A GREEK LEGEND

One day the handsome youth Narcissus looked into a clear mountain pool. He fell in love with the face he saw, not realizing that it was his own reflection.

Narcissus could not win the love of the person in the pool and died of sorrow. He then turned into the flower named for him. Today we say that a person is *narcissistic* if he admires himself too much.

MIRROR OF KINGS

Across the centuries, some mirrors have been credited with magic powers. A famous magic mirror was made by sorcerers (magicians) for Catherine de Medici (1519-1589), Queen of France. In this mirror, she supposedly could see the future rulers of France.

The first mirrors were probably quiet ponds. When a man looked into a pond and saw his image, smooth and unruffled, it was a sign that the gods would be good to him. But if the image was broken and distorted by ripples, there was trouble ahead.

Mirror images are clear unless the mirror is cracked. Originally, the image itself was thought to foretell the future. As time passed, the cracked mirror rather than the image became the sign of bad luck.

3 plus 4

Why is a cracked mirror supposed to cause 7 years' bad luck? Seven is a special number that for thousands of years has meant either good or bad luck. Its supposed magic dates back to early superstitious beliefs about the numbers 3 and 4. Once numbers were more than signs for counting all sorts of quantities. They also represented specific things or ideas.

Today we generally do not identify the number 3 with anything in particular; it is used to count books, fruit, bicycles, and so on. But to some ancient peoples, like the Egyptians, the number 3 represented the Mother, Father, and Son. These 3, called a *trinity*, were regarded as the basis for continuing life from one generation to the next.

In time, the number 3 came to represent something more than the continuation of life. Since life was mysterious and spiritual, the number 3 grew to mean the spirit or mind of man.

The number 4 represented the 4 chief directions — north, south, east, and west. Earth was then believed to be square. The number 4 and the 4 directions it represented were shown as a small square that looked like a house.

Three and 4 were combined to produce the sacred number 7. Small wonder that 7 is connected with so many superstitions! It once stood for an immensely powerful idea: the house that contains the spirit of man.

SPIRITS OF THE GODS

A few thousand years ago, Egyptians believed that the spirit of a god was inside its statue. Some gods were human in form. Others had the heads of animals or were completely animal.

When a Pharaoh was crowned, he became a descendant of Horus, the hawk — god of the sun. Horus is shown here protecting the Pharaoh Nectanebos, who ruled Egypt in 350 B.C.

Sekhmet, the goddess of war, was a woman with the head of a lioness. In one hand, she held the ankh, a special cross that represented life. The ankh still has the same meaning today.

9

THE 7 AGES OF MAN

One of the most famous sevens in literature is in a speech in William Shakespeare's *As You Like It*. The speech begins:

All the world's a stage,
And all the men and women
merely players.
They have their exits and
their entrances;
And one man in his time
plays many parts,
His acts being seven ages.

Shakespeare then describes these ages, which are listed below and shown in the drawings.

infant

schoolboy

lover

soldier

justice

older man

very old man

10

Sevens everywhere

Let us look at a few of the superstitions involving the number 7. A seventh child is supposed to be lucky. In the United States, Scotland, and some other countries, he is also thought to have the power to heal the sick. In Rumanian legends, however, a seventh child is unlucky. He is doomed, after death, to turn into a vampire, a creature that rises from its grave at night. Gypsies also have faith in the magic 7. They believe that the seventh daughter of a seventh daughter will become a great fortune teller.

The Bible, too, mentions 7 frequently — for example, 7 days of Creation, 7 years of plenty and 7 years of famine, 7 stars, 7 golden candlesticks, 7 lamps of fire, a book sealed with 7 seals, a lamb with 7 horns and 7 eyes, 7 angels with 7 trumpets, and a dragon with 7 heads.

Even among those Americans who are not too superstitious, the number 7 is considered lucky whenever it appears. Just think how pleased some people are (you, too?) when they find one or more sevens in ordinary numbers like these: a street address, an automobile license plate, a telephone number, a seat number, or a locker number.

In numbers connected with sports, 7 stands out even more as a sign of luck. Imagine that you are watching a baseball game. It is the seventh inning, and the team you are rooting for is losing. Many of the people who want that team to win — fans and players alike — will be saying to themselves and perhaps out loud, "This is the lucky seventh."

A sneezer's spirit

After a sneeze, someone is bound to say, "God bless you" or "Gesundheit," which is German and has come to mean about the same thing. An Italian will say "Salute" and a Frenchman "Que Dieu vous bénisse." This superstition of offering a blessing or expressing a hope for good health is widespread. Why? No one offers a blessing for a cough or hiccup. A sneeze is no more serious than a cough.

GUARDING THE BRIDE
In China 100 years ago, a bride and her husband would visit her parents on the third day of their marriage. The coach they traveled in often was painted with a picture of a great magician riding a tiger. With raised sword, the magician was ready to drive away any evil spirits that intended to harm the bride.

CURE FOR ILLNESS
When a man was very sick, his spirit left his body, according to an old Chinese belief. The spirit had to return in order for the man to recover.

A member of the family would take a coat belonging to the sick man and hang it on the end of a bamboo pole. Between the pole and the coat, a metal mirror was placed in the position of a head.

It was hoped that the spirit would come into the coat. If this occurred, the bamboo pole was said to sometimes turn slowly. The coat was placed over the sick man so that the spirit could re-enter the body and bring back good health.

Gesundheit has nothing to do with the possibility that a sneezer may be coming down with a cold. Our special attitude towards sneezing comes from a time when men believed that a person's spirit, or soul, resided in his head.

A man living thousands of years ago felt that his spirit was as real as he was. A good hard sneeze might blow it right out of his head. Before the sneezer's spirit could get back, some evil spirit that was lurking around might get into his head first. So when a man sneezed, all his friends would say a prayer or bless him to keep the evil spirit away.

How to scare a spirit

When you sneeze, you are supposed to cover your nose with a handkerchief. This is just good sense because a sneeze can spread germs. But why are you supposed to cover your mouth when you yawn? Not to do so is considered very rude, yet yawning spreads few or no germs. This custom, too, started thousands of years ago. At that time, a man was afraid that his spirit might escape through his open mouth or that some evil spirit might enter. So he blocked his mouth with his hand. In modern times, this ancient belief has been changed. Some parents tell their children to cover their mouths when they yawn, or a fly might get in.

We clink glasses before we drink a toast. This custom also traces back to a superstitious fear of evil spirits. One might enter your mouth while you were drinking, so it seemed best to frighten it away with a noise. At one time, the noises were very loud; for example, in some countries, it was traditional to fire a cannon when the king drank. We now settle for a simple clink of glasses.

Salt over your left shoulder

Why is it considered bad luck to spill salt at the table? Salt is cheap and easy to clean up. It would seem much worse luck to spill something like soup, which makes a mess. Salt is necessary in our diet. Although we can obtain it easily now, many ancient peoples had a hard time getting enough. They considered salt extremely valuable and therefore bad luck to waste.

If you spill salt, you may be advised to throw a pinch of it over your left shoulder. This ancient practice, still in use, is supposed to drive away evil spirits. Why over your left shoulder? Left is considered unlucky or evil, a place where evil spirits hover. Our word *sinister*, meaning wicked or evil, is the Latin word for *left*.

The high esteem in which people once held salt is heard in common sayings in our language. We talk of a man, "not being worth his salt." When we are not sure whether to believe something, we "take it with a grain of salt." Once salt was believed to have all sorts of wonderful powers. For instance, the Greeks placed salt on a newborn baby's tongue to assure the baby a safe future and good health. Another ancient belief was that salt sprinkled in the doorway of a new home would keep away evil spirits. Most such beliefs have disappeared over the centuries. But the two just described are still practiced by some superstitious people.

**PAYMENT
AND PRESERVATIVE**
Roman soldiers were supplied with salt or given money to buy it.

In those times, salt was an important preservative. A superstition developed that an agreement would be more lasting if the people involved ate a meal containing salt.

Even today the Iranian expression "untrue to salt" indicates a broken promise or disloyalty.

**LITTLE CHANGE
IN ANCIENT METHODS**
In some regions of the world, salt is still mined and transported as it was a few thousand years ago, as shown here in Ceylon. Several salt mines in northern India have been worked from a time before Alexander the Great (356-323 B.C.).

HAIR BRACELET

In the middle of the 19th century, bracelets made of hair (like the one in the photograph) were popular. The hair usually came from the wearer or somebody close to her. The bracelets were supposed to bring good luck and sometimes became family heirlooms.

Saving a baby tooth

In some families when a child loses a baby tooth, it is hidden under his pillow. At one time, the tooth was salted and then burned. It was also common once to save a lock of a child's hair, and many parents still do so. Such customs, which involve the teeth and the hair, have fearful origins.

Primitive peoples often believed that all parts of the body are magically connected. Thus if an enemy obtained a lost tooth or a lock of hair, he could gain magic power over the person they came from. For that reason, parents were always careful to gather up all of a child's hair after his first haircut and all of his lost baby teeth. The hair and teeth were hidden or destroyed because an evil person might find them and gain power over the child.

Fortunately, many superstitions today are harmless. Some have even become pleasant rather than frightening. Parents may tell their children about a fairy who will take the lost tooth left under the pillow and leave a coin in its place. The lock of a child's hair that is saved usually becomes a souvenir of childhood, along with baby shoes and photographs.

What will tomorrow bring?

Even in America and other nations where most people have been educated, some still allow superstition rather than reason to guide their lives. One widespread superstition today is the belief in *astrology* — an ancient method of attempting to foretell the future by studying the position of the sun, moon, stars, and planets. It is based on the idea that these heavenly bodies influence the character and future of men and women on earth.

Astrology was born when little was known about the heavens. It was thought that the gods guided the movements of the heavens as they guided the movements of men. Therefore, it seemed logical that the heavens and men's lives should somehow be related. Astrologers came into being and developed elaborate methods for interpreting the sky.

ZODIAC SYMBOLS
Believers in astrology often carry with them the symbol of their zodiac sign. The rings in the photograph show all 12 symbols.

Circle in the heavens

Astrologers created the *zodiac* by dividing a circular band of the sky into 12 equal parts. Each part, or *sign*, contained a constellation (cluster of stars). The sign was named for the figure that astrologers saw in the pattern of stars in the constellation.

ASK A COMPUTER
Those who believe that their fate can be foretold by the stars can now ask a computer for the information.

Each month about 15,000 Americans obtain a computer horoscope for $20 from some 350 department stores.

The horoscope, in the form of a written report, discusses such items as character, romance, health, and the future.

Aries, the Ram	Mar 21 through Apr 19
Taurus, the Bull	Apr 20 through May 20
Gemini, the Twins	May 21 through Jun 21
Cancer, the Crab	Jun 22 through Jul 22
Leo, the Lion	Jul 23 through Aug 22
Virgo, the Virgin	Aug 23 through Sep 22
Libra, the Scales	Sep 23 through Oct 22
Scorpio, the Scorpion	Oct 23 through Nov 21
Sagittarius, the Archer	Nov 22 through Dec 21
Capricorn, the Goat	Dec 22 through Jan 19
Aquarius, the Water Bearer	Jan 20 through Feb 18
Pisces, the Fishes	Feb 19 through Mar 20

The constellations are no longer in the same place in the zodiac because of our shifting view of the heavens over thousands of years.

The 9th sign of the zodiac, Sagittarius, the Archer, is in the Southern Hemisphere. Early astrologers saw in this cluster of stars the form of a centaur holding a bow and arrow. The centaur was a creature in Greek myths who was part man and part horse.

"DARLING, ACCORDING TO YOUR HOROSCOPE THIS IS YOUR LUCKY DAY!"

Each sign of the zodiac is supposed to influence a certain time of the year. According to astrologers, a person's future can be forecast by calculating the position of the heavenly bodies at a particular time. Such forecasts are called *horoscopes*.

About 5 out of 7 daily newspapers carry horoscope columns. Each morning millions of readers hope to find what the day has in store for them. Or they hope to learn how they should act in order to have the day turn out favorably. Newspaper horoscopes are generally vague, and a reader can often interpret them any way he wants. Here is a typical horoscope from a daily newspaper:

> You can expect others to be less demanding today. The time is right for increased social activities. Travel is favorable. Watch out for gossip.

If you look at a newspaper horoscope, you will see that each of the 12 signs is listed with a starting and ending date, like the table on page 15. To find your horoscope, select the sign your birthday falls in.

No 2 people alike

We can see how vague newspaper horoscopes are by using simple division as a tool. Let us assume that you were born March 2. You will find your horoscope under the sign for February 20 through March 20. Now let us see how many other people have the same horoscope. More than 3½ billion people live in the world. There are 12 different horoscopes in the newspaper column, each corresponding to a different sign of the zodiac. If we divide 3½ billion by 12, we find that approximately 300 million people have the same horoscope. (We have assumed that the same number of babies is born under each sign. Actually, differences exist, but they are not large enough to be important in this example.)

One of the wonders of life is that no 2 people are alike. Does it seem reasonable, then, that you and 300 million others should be receiving the same advice? If you think of all the people you know — and how different their personalities and problems are — the answer seems clear.

Some people who believe in astrology are not satisfied with newspaper horoscopes. They frequently spend large sums of money to have astrologers prepare personal horoscopes for them. It is not unusual for such people to allow astrologers to guide them in making important decisions.

Astrology became less believable

The astrologers' view of the universe flourished in the ancient countries of Babylonia, Egypt, China, and India. It spread into Rome and the West about the time that Christianity began. In Europe, astrology grew and became an important study during the *Middle Ages*, a period of approximately 1,000 years, from about the 5th to the 15th century.

As the work of great scientists like Galileo Galilei (1564-1642) and Johannes Kepler (1571-1630) spread, astrology became less believable. The more men learned about the universe, the more they realized that the positions of the heavenly bodies did not decide their fate. The astrologers' belief that the skies influence human life is hundreds of years behind the times. Today, most people who have a scientific approach consider astrology to be pure superstition. Yet a large number of people — often intelligent and well educated — read their daily horoscopes and consult astrologers for guidance.

EARLY MEXICAN ASTROLOGY
Astrology was important in the everyday life of the Aztec Indians, of Mexico. Unfortunately, most Aztec writings, including their astrology signs (picture), were destroyed by Spanish conquerers during the 16th century.

SHAKESPEARE'S *HAMLET*

In a celebrated scene from the play, Hamlet meets and talks with his father's ghost. But Hamlet fears that the ghost is a demon posing as his father. To protect himself, he holds his sword like a cross. The ghost reassures Hamlet, saying:

I am thy father's spirit,
Doomed for a certain term
to walk the night,

The belief that the cross is a protection against evil goes back long before the birth of the Christian religion. The cross, in one or another of its ancient forms, is a few thousand years older than Christianity.

Fear of ghosts

Primitive men were deeply afraid of *ghosts* — that is, the spirits of dead people. When somebody dies, what happens to his spirit? they wondered. One reasonable answer was that the spirit remains near the place where the person's body is buried. The custom of putting a tombstone on a grave comes from this belief. Today the tombstone is used as a memorial to a dead person. But once people rolled a heavy stone on top of a grave to keep the ghost from getting out.

As people learned more about the world, they began to doubt that ghosts are real. Throughout the centuries, many different tests have been devised to see if ghosts exist. No one has ever been able to prove that they do — and most of us have concluded that there are no ghosts.

But ghostly superstitions linger on. Many people feel a little nervous when passing a graveyard at night. There is even a superstition that whistling near a graveyard will ward off ghosts. Few of us would care to spend a night alone in a house that had a reputation for being haunted, even if we did not believe in ghosts. Indeed, some houses that are supposed to be haunted are difficult to sell or rent.

Unreasonable fear

Being afraid of ghosts, even when we tend not to believe in them, may cause us a few unpleasant moments. But the fear is not a problem unless it becomes extreme. Then it is called a *phobia* — an unreasonable and continuing fear of a particular thing or situation. For example, a person who will never pass a graveyard under any condition — night or day, with or without friends — is considered to have a phobia about graveyards.

People have phobias about objects, animals, other people, events, and situations. Since all of these can also cause fear, what is the difference between fear and phobia?

The answer is that whatever causes a phobia is not truly dangerous. Consider a person who will not go near any dog. If he is afraid of a large, wild dog, his fear is reasonable. However, if he is also afraid of a 3-day-old puppy, his fear is unreasonable, and he has a phobia.

People who talk to spirits

Some people are quite serious about ghosts and spirits — yet they do not have phobias. In a way, the opposite is true. Instead of fearing spirits, they try to contact the spirit world. Usually they ask for the help of a *medium,* a person who claims to link the spirit world with our world by transmitting messages back and forth. Many mediums are frauds and cheat people out of large sums of money.

Not all mediums, however, practice deceit. Some really believe that they are in touch with the dead. Often a medium will fall into a *trance,* a sleeplike state where she is not aware of what is going on around her. (Mediums are usually, but not always, women.) While in a trance she will start to speak. Sometimes her trance voice will sound very different from her usual voice. When she awakens, the medium will not remember what she said while she was in the trance.

The supernatural world

Mediums claim that during a trance their bodies are *possessed* — taken over and controlled by a spirit. Trances

NO FEAR OF GHOSTS
On a sunny day, Trinity churchyard, in New York City, is crowded with office workers relaxing during lunch hour.

Some of the people may believe in ghosts, and others may not. But nobody seems too concerned because ghosts usually are not thought of as daytime creatures.

An old superstition holds that ghosts become restless only at night. Then a ghost supposedly rises from its burial place and wanders about, sometimes haunting the scene of its death.

Such beliefs are based on fears of the unknown that linger from the past. One day they will probably disappear as did the superstition that diseases are caused by evil spirits.

19

THE CAMERA ALWAYS TELLS THE TRUTH — OR DOES IT?

A skillful photographer can create many illusions. He can even make the supernatural look believable. Both ghosts seem real, for example; but they are not.

Almost 100 years separate these examples of trick photography. The photograph above was taken when photography was in its infancy. The one on the left was made for this book.

and possession played a very important role in the religions of primitive peoples. The body of a person in a trance was believed to have been entered by gods or spirits. Today we know that at least some people who are in a trance may have hypnotized themselves.

The supernatural world, for those who believe in it, is inhabited by ghosts and spirits — who, on occasion, are supposed to visit mediums. The word *supernatural* is often heard in discussions about superstitions. *Super* is Latin for *above* or *outside*. Putting *super* and *natural* together, we obtain the meaning of *supernatural:* outside the known laws and forces of nature.

As we can see from our investigation so far, which has ranged from missing 13th floors to mediums, the supernatural world is still very much with us today. Yet most of us no longer live in a world ruled by superstitious fears of the unknown. Although millions of people still consult astrologers and newspaper horoscopes, we have learned enough of *astronomy,* the real science of the heavens, to have landed men on the moon.

Chapter 2

WHEN WE IGNORE HABIT OR RITUAL OR SUPERSTITION

Can an animal be superstitious? Let us follow the great Austrian student of animal behavior Dr. Konrad Lorenz to find an answer. However, we have to get in line, for Dr. Lorenz has another pursuer. Between us and Dr. Lorenz — trailing him and hurrying to keep up — is a European graylag goose.

Developing a habit

Dr. Lorenz had raised the graylag goose, which he named Martina, from an egg. The goose followed him everywhere, even up to his bedroom at night. The first time the young goose followed him upstairs she was only a week old. Climbing the stairs was a new and frightening experience for her.

The little goose ran to a window near the staircase and sat in the light for a few moments until she calmed down. Then she walked back to Dr. Lorenz and followed him upstairs. The next night she acted the same way, although her pause at the window was shorter.

MORE THAN CLEANLINESS
Baboons groom each other, removing lice and dirt. Some zoologists say that grooming is more than an act of hygiene. It is also a social ritual.

As a ritual, grooming can be considered a series of acts that permits the baboons to rely on and serve one another. Thus they are able to live together better than they might otherwise.

22

Within a few days, she gave up stopping at the window altogether. But she still ran toward it. "She no longer gave the impression of being frightened. The detour acquired more and more the character of a habit," wrote Dr. Lorenz. A *habit* is an act that is repeated so often that it occurs almost automatically — that is, without thought.

Fear of breaking a habit

One night Dr. Lorenz forgot to let Martina into the house until long past the usual hour. When he finally opened the front door, the anxious goose ran right through his legs and up the stairs without making her usual turn toward the window. When Martina reached the fifth step, she suddenly stopped and uttered a warning cry.

Then the frightened goose turned around, ran hurriedly down the steps, "and set forth resolutely, like someone on a very important mission, on her original path to the window and back." After completing her accustomed route, she climbed the stairs with obvious signs of relief.

Dr. Lorenz was astonished. "I hardly believed my eyes. To me there is no doubt about the interpretation of this occurrence: the habit had become a custom which the goose could not break without being stricken by fear." The goose had become superstitious about turning toward the window before going upstairs.

The scientist compared the goose's superstitious behavior with his own. "I remember clearly that as a child, I had persuaded myself that something terrible would happen if I stepped on one of the lines instead of into the squares of the paving stones."

The superstition about stepping on a line is widespread. It is even part of a game called "lines and squares." If you are playing the game, you can feel very uneasy if you step on a line. A children's rhyme, "Step on a crack, break your mother's back," is sometimes chanted by the players.

A bedtime story

We have said that a habit is an act that is repeated so often that it occurs almost automatically. This descrip-

TOWARD THE LIGHT
Dr. Lorenz reported: "As Martina, following obediently at my heels, walked into the hall, the unaccustomed situation suddenly filled her with terror and she strove, as frightened birds always do, toward the light."

SUPERSTITIOUS WALKER
Many young people believe that stepping on a crack brings bad luck. This superstition does not always disappear with maturity. Some older people avoid stepping on a crack for the same reason.

23

PEACOCK RITUAL

During mating season, male peacocks perform a courtship ritual. When a male wants to display interest in a female, he spreads his tail like a spectacular fan and walks about in a dance.

How do human and animal rituals differ? Perhaps the most important difference is this: Human rituals change and develop, but animal rituals tend to remain the same.

tion sometimes applies to another term that is helpful in understanding superstitions — *ritual*. Brushing one's teeth regularly is called a habit by some people, a ritual by others. However, in this book, we will consider a *ritual* to be a series of acts that are part of a ceremony.

For example, a wedding, the launching of a ship, graduation exercises, and the awarding of a prize are rituals. Though most rituals are part of such formal occasions, they need not be. Even a bedtime story can develop into a ritual to a small child.

If the storytelling ritual is broken, the child can become very upset. Many children prefer to hear the same story over and over again. The story has no surprises left, for they know every word of it. Thus these children are soothed by the story more than they are entertained by it.

Anxiety

What happens if the storyteller changes the story for variety? Some children may become anxious and have difficulty going to sleep. *Anxiety* is a vague feeling of fear and nervousness. Often an anxious person, child or adult, does not know exactly what is troubling him.

Anxiety, as we are beginning to see, plays a role in many situations, superstitious and otherwise. We already noted that the goose behaved in a superstitious manner. A person who avoids stepping on a line is certainly superstitious. But what about the child who feels anxious when his bedtime ritual is changed?

Some people would say that his behavior was like that of the goose and therefore superstitious. However, most psychologists (scientists who study human behavior) do not think of young children as being superstitious. They would describe the child as being anxious, or in a state of anxiety.

Completing a ritual

Let us look now at what happened when an adult bedtime ritual was changed. A young man worked on a job where it was important that he get to work early and on time. He developed a ritual of checking his alarm clock 3 or 4 times before going to sleep.

Then he went to work on a new job where it did not matter if he were on time in the morning. Yet he continued to worry about checking the alarm clock even though it was no longer necessary. If he omitted the usual ritual, he became nervous and had trouble falling asleep. His anxiety was caused by his failure to complete a ritual that had turned into a superstition.

A superstitious person may experience anxiety when he fails to knock wood or throw a pinch of salt over his shoulder. Even if he thinks the ritual is meaningless, he will feel uncomfortable if he does not complete it. He may explain his superstitious belief by saying, "Well, what is there to lose? And besides, you never know what might happen."

HANGING ON

In the cartoon *Peanuts*, the young boy Linus likes his teacher, Miss Othmar. But he has an even stronger attachment to his blanket. When he chooses between the two — the blanket wins.

Such attachments often are based on rituals or superstitions that cause distress when they are not followed. As we have seen:

- The child became upset when the story was changed.

- The young man became upset when he stopped checking the alarm clock.

- And Linus once said: "I can't live without that blanket. I can't face life unarmed."

PEANUTS ®   **By Charles M. Schulz**

HELPFUL SPIRIT

In the legends of the Hopi and other Pueblo Indians, *kachinas* are spirits who help humanity at times.

When kachinas leave the spirit world and visit the earth, they can bestow such benefits as good health and good crops. Kachinas, therefore, play an important role in the rituals of the Pueblo people of the American Southwest.

Carved kachina dolls, like the one shown in the photograph, represent individual spirits and are given to children.

RIGHT FOOT FORWARD
An old sea superstition states that a sailor should step on-to a ship making its first voyage with his right foot.

This superstition still lin-gers. It is also heard for dif-ferent situations in the ex-pression: "Get off to a good start with your right foot."

Some superstitious people are more direct. They feel that their beliefs help them in specific ways. In this, they are like primitive people, who have rituals for almost everything that is important to them, for instance, bringing rain, winning battles, and preserving their health.

Is the ritual itself at fault?

Events do not always turn out the way primitive men or men in our own civilization want them to. The more elaborate the ritual, the easier it is to excuse failure. It is not difficult to find some place in an elaborate ritual that went wrong. Thus the performance of the ritual rather than the ritual itself can be blamed.

For example, the Aymara Indians of Peru have an age-old ritual for making rain in times of drought. The ritual involves frogs, water plants, prayers, the playing of pipes and drums, a singing chorus, and a trip to a mountain. A lot can go wrong with so many parts to the rainmaking ritual. If rain does not come, the failure can be excused by claiming that one part of the ritual was not properly performed. The people believe that when the rainmaking ritual is carried out correctly, it works well. Otherwise, it would not have lasted for centuries.

THE LOWER THE BOW ...
Bowing is a ritual of greeting and respect in Japan. Like all rituals, this one has details that an outsider may not recognize.

For example, the level of the bow is important. In the photograph, the 2 women bow deeply as a tribute to the age and position of the woman at the right.

Why we shake hands

We sometimes think of rituals as empty, foolish, and occasionally harmful. Some of them are. But we must also recognize that many rituals serve an important purpose. They help people get along with one another. Groups of people probably could not live together if they did not share certain rituals.

Consider the handshake. We think of it as a friendly act, but it did not start that way. You have probably seen a western movie or television show where two rivals agree to meet. Before they enter the same room, they are forced to check their guns at the door. Well, the origins of the handshake are just about that friendly.

When men carried swords, approaching another man with your right hand held out was a sign that you meant him no harm. (Possibly the custom started back in the time when men carried clubs.) An open right hand showed the other man that your weapon hand was empty. Then you firmly grasped his outstretched right hand to make sure that he could not suddenly reach for his weapon. The handshake began as a sign of mutual distrust between two warriors. To this day, men shake hands more than women.

If you stop shaking hands

The handshake is a ritual that has lost its original purpose. Should shaking hands, therefore, be regarded as a modern superstitious ritual? Probably not, because handshaking has taken on a new meaning.

Over the centuries, handshaking developed into a ritual that expresses friendship and good wishes. At its least, it is a way of saying hello. If you suddenly decided that shaking hands was meaningless and that you were not going to shake hands anymore, people would think you were being unfriendly. Even if you explained your reasons, they would still feel that you disliked them because you did not want to share in this universal ritual of greeting.

The Christmas tree

Let us look at a few of the rituals that surround Christmas, the holiday that celebrates the birth of Jesus Christ. Many Christmas rituals, like those involving the Christmas tree, originally were not part of Christian custom.

The Christmas tree dates all the way back to pagan times. Then, long before Christ was born, many people worshiped gods of nature, like the sun god. To these pagans, light and the green of the tree were signs of hope that, even in winter, nature was not dead. Mistletoe and

TURNAROUND
The straw goat still appears in Sweden at Christmas time, as it did centuries ago. Then the goat represented the Devil and evil powers in plays and other Christmas rituals.

In time, these rituals disappeared, but the goat remained. Today it is a Christmas decoration and stands for the good things of the holiday season. It serves as an example that rituals can change and even reverse their meaning.

29

holly, 2 other plants that stay green throughout the year, were also used in midwinter pagan festivals.

Saint Nicholas, whom we now know as Santa Claus, originally had no connection with Christmas. He lived about 300 years after Christ and became a bishop of the Church. Saint Nicholas was known in his time and in later legends for giving gifts. It is easy to see why he became associated with Christmas, since the exchange of gifts adds to the spirit and joy of the season.

Friendly rituals

Some Christmas rituals have been criticized for being too commercial, that is, having profit rather than religion or friendship as their foundation. Yet, somehow or other, commercial or not, Christmas usually turns out to be a great happy holiday. The sharing of rituals — trimming the tree, sending cards, exchanging presents, eating with relatives and friends — binds people together. This brief period is, for many people, the friendliest time of the year.

The friendly rituals of Christmas are often customs that are connected with the holiday; they are not actually part of the official beliefs of any Christian church. For example, as we have said, evergreens and lights — from torches, oil lamps, and bonfires — were used in pagan festivals to show that life continued through the winter. Most people who place lights on Christmas trees are copying the ancient pagan ritual without quite knowing why. However, people today do not just follow this ritual without any reason. It is likely that we share with those who lived thousands of years ago the feeling that a tree and lights are a cheerful and festive sight.

We have seen, in this chapter, that some superstitions grow out of habit and ritual. Further, we have learned what happens when men and animals ignore habit or ritual or superstition. They sometimes develop troubled, or anxious, feelings. We have discovered, too, that some modern rituals began many years ago as superstitions. Or they originally may have had another purpose, like the safety of a handshake. Today, these rituals do not serve us in the exact same way they did our ancestors. But they are still valuable — perhaps more than ever — because they often help us to live with one another in greater friendship.

SONGS AND FOOD

These are part of many different holiday rituals everywhere. In Germany, children dressed as The Three Kings sing Christmas carols in the snow-covered streets. They are often rewarded with good things to eat, like dolls that have walnut heads and plum bodies.

31

Chapter 3
SYMPATHETIC MAGIC

Magic is an attempt to control events by means that we now know are supernatural, that is, outside the known laws of nature. But man did not always think that magic was beyond nature. At one time, magic seemed as logical and practical as science does today. Many of our superstitions come from the time when magic was an everyday part of life.

Like produces like

The oldest and simplest form of magic we know of is called *sympathetic magic*. When he attempts sympathetic magic, a magician tries to control some distant object or person. He can work with 2 principles. Both are quite reasonable in a world where scientific thinking and testing are unknown. We must realize that the primitive magician was not necessarily less intelligent than the modern scientist — he simply had fewer facts at his command.

CAVE SUPERSTITION IN A LIVING ROOM
If the picture is placed upside down, the man will feel distress, according to a superstition based on sympathetic magic. In prehistoric times, the same kind of thinking produced drawings of wounded animals on cave walls (next page).

MAGIC ART
Some 16,000 years ago, this animal was drawn on the wall of a cave in southern France. It is pierced by a weapon. Probably the artist hoped that tribal hunters would have similar good luck through the magic of "like produces like."

Animals were sometimes drawn without ears. Why? As with many questions based on events thousands of years old, we do not have a definite answer. A reasonable guess, however, is that animals that did not have ears would not hear the hunters.

The first principle of sympathetic magic is "like produces like." The earliest examples of this type of magic appear in the drawings of cave men. We now believe that the artists were also magicians and that the drawings were not meant to be decorations. They were usually made deep in caves where few people would ever see them. Some of the drawings show animals pierced with arrows or caught in traps.

The purpose of the drawings, according to many modern scholars, was magical. If the magician-artist drew a deer pierced by hunters' arrows, he believed that when the tribe's real hunters went out, they would magically repeat the scene — like produces like.

The magic connection

The second principle of sympathetic magic is that things that were once in contact always retain a magic connection with one another. In chapter 1, we saw an example of this principle: Primitive men were afraid that they would be harmed if cut hair or lost teeth fell into the hands of an enemy.

Blood was considered to be a particularly powerful agent of magic. Pacts signed in blood were supposed to have a special and awesome significance. In the folklore of Europe, pacts with the Devil had to be signed in blood. Men sometimes swore to become "blood brothers." In this ceremony, two friends would each cut a finger or hand and press the wounds together. The exchange of

PACT WITH THE DEVIL
This document was offered as evidence against a French priest accused of witchcraft in 1634. It was supposed to be a pact between the priest and the Devil and his chief assistants.

The devils state that the priest "will offer to us once a year a tribute marked with his blood." On such superstitious evidence and the testimony of witnesses who later admitted they were lying, the priest was convicted and killed.

33

blood gave each "brother" magic power over the other and insured loyalty.

Often the 2 principles of sympathetic magic are combined. In *voodoo,* a religion that still flourishes in some parts of the West Indies, a voodoo priest will, on occasion, make a doll to resemble a person over whom he wishes to have magic power. But the doll has no magic power, supposedly, unless the priest can obtain some hair clippings, or the like, from his intended victim. These are mixed with the wax of the doll.

The magic of bravery

The African hunter who proudly wears the mane of a lion he has killed, or the Malay hunter with a necklace of tiger's teeth, or the American Indian with a headdress of eagle feathers are also appealing to sympathetic magic. Lions, tigers, and eagles are admired for their bravery by the men who hunt them. By wearing something from one of these creatures, a hunter hopes to magically gain some of its bravery.

An act like cannibalism, which we consider savagery, must be viewed with an understanding of sympathetic magic. The cannibal is not an inhuman monster. When he eats the flesh of an opponent, he expects the dead man's bravery to be magically transferred to him.

Is modern man immune to the attractions of sympathetic magic? No, he is not. During World War II, for example, the group of airmen called the Flying Tigers painted the noses of their aircraft with tooth-filled shark mouths. Further back, on the body of each plane, they also painted a savage-looking tiger. Of course, the pilots did not believe that the pictures themselves were magical. But remember that like produces like — so that sharks and tigers could help create a mood for battle, perhaps making some pilots feel fiercer and braver.

SYMPATHETIC MAGIC FROM MASKS

Masks of animals were used by North American Indians and Eskimos for many purposes — for example, to acquire some desirable quality of the animal.

In this form of sympathetic magic, a believer could hope to gain strength from the mask of the bear (left); savage courage from the mask of the eagle (above); and hunting skill from the mask of the wolf (right).

35

MAGIC THAT FLOWS THROUGH A STICK

The magic wand is the most famous of the magician's tools. It may trace back to the staff, which is a long stick or pole.

At various times, a staff has been a sign of authority, a weapon, and an object of magic. For example:

Pictures of St. Peter show him with a staff. On ceremonial occasions, ancient kings carried scepters (staffs) as signs of power. Moses struck a rock with his staff, in the biblical story, and water flowed.

No accidents

As we have said, magic to the primitive man was a force of nature. With proper techniques, a magician could transfer magic power from one place to another — just as an electrician can transfer electric power between two locations. Magic power could also be stored in objects in the same way that electric power can be stored in a battery.

Quite early in man's history he began to carry a variety of *charms, talismans, amulets,* and *fetishes.* All of these terms have slightly different meanings to the deeply superstitious person. But in everyday language, they are used interchangeably. They describe an object that is supposed to contain some form of magic or be the residence of a friendly spirit.

Primitive man did not believe in accidents. There had to be a reason for everything. Evil spirits or evil magicians made bad things happen, and good spirits or friendly magicians made good things happen. The world of magic is orderly and logical for those who believe in it. Carrying a charm in such a world is as normal as having a vaccination in ours.

The rabbit's foot

A few people still carry charms to protect them from evil spirits or hostile magic. Many more, however, carry the opposite kind of charm, one that is supposed to bring good luck. The purpose of a good luck charm is to make accidental events work out favorably. Of course, a belief in good luck charms is just as superstitious as the older belief in charms against evil.

The most popular good luck charm is the rabbit's foot. If you have ever owned one, you may have been asked, "Why do you carry a rabbit's foot? It wasn't lucky for the rabbit." Your questioner may have been having fun, but he also had a point.

Today the rabbit's foot is worn on a keychain or carried in the pocket. In years past, however, the rabbit's foot had additional uses. For example, it was once customary to brush a newborn baby with a rabbit's foot so that some of the charm's luck would rub off on the baby. Often a young actor would be given a rabbit's foot before his

LUCKY BEETLE

A scarab is a beetle of the Mediterranean area. Carvings of this insect (left), also called scarabs, were used as charms in Egypt as far back as 5,000 years ago.

Scarabs came to represent the force that made the sun come to life again each day and cross the heavens. Generally they were regarded as luck pieces.

They were also placed in Egyptian tombs to help the soul of the dead person be reborn — just as the sun is reborn when it rises.

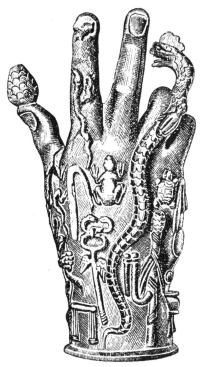

ANCIENT EGYPTIAN CHARM

This bronze hand is covered with magic symbols that are supposed to provide protection against evil — for example, a pine cone, a frog, and a serpent with a rooster's comb.

TO MAKE MONEY GROW

Both sides of a Chinese lucky charm are shown in the photograph (right). Such charms were often placed by shopkeepers in their money boxes. The writing means "one to make ten thousand" — a request to the gods of luck for the money to grow.

"THE ONLY THING BROKEN WAS YOUR RABBIT'S FOOT!"

first performance. He was supposed to apply makeup with it for the rest of his career. If he lost the rabbit's foot, good luck would desert him.

Why was the rabbit so special?

We can only speculate on how the rabbit's foot charm started. It may have come down to us from primitive man. Some primitive tribes believed that they were descended from animals. The particular animal that was considered the ancestor of the tribe is called its *totem*. Often a tribesman would carry part of the totem animal as a charm. It is not too hard to imagine that a primitive hunter might consider his rabbit's foot charm as important as his spear.

The custom of carrying a protective rabbit's foot probably persisted long after the belief in totem animals disappeared. Why was the mild-mannered rabbit so special? We have only bits of evidence to help us find the answer.

For instance, during the Middle Ages, people regarded the rabbit with superstitious awe because of its habit of burrowing into the ground. They wondered what it might be doing down there — perhaps communicating with the spirits of the underworld. Such fears helped keep alive a belief in the supernatural powers of the rabbit.

The rabbit's well-known fertility (ability to have many young) further added to the popularity of the rabbit's foot charm. When farming dominated man's activities, fertility was respected and even worshiped. Farmers wanted large crops, many farm animals, and big families to help with the work. The fertile rabbit was an excellent choice to represent abundance and good luck.

How to hang a horseshoe

If you find a horseshoe and hang it above your doorway, the superstition goes, you will have good luck. Most people hang a horseshoe the easiest way, with the open end pointed down. But a truly superstitious person would never hang a horseshoe that way. He believes that a horseshoe must be hung with the open end pointed up; otherwise, the luck will run out. This idea comes from the superstition that a charm itself is not important — what counts is the helpful spirit or magic that the charm contains.

The origins of the horseshoe superstition are lost in legend. One story is that the superstition began in the 10th century, when Saint Dunstan, a blacksmith, trapped the Devil. He made the Evil One promise never to enter a house that had a horseshoe over the door.

However, the superstition is probably much older than Christianity. The ancient Romans hammered nails on the outside of their doors in the belief that metal could keep away evil. The horseshoe itself may have come to be considered lucky because of its resemblance to the crescent moon, an important sign of good luck. Witches were supposed to fear horses — that is why they rode broomsticks. The horseshoe could have been a charm for keeping witches out of the home.

Find one for luck

Another powerful charm of good luck is the 4 leaf clover. All sorts of 4 leaf clover charms are sold. But the only way to really obtain luck from a 4 leaf clover, according to superstition, is to find it yourself, preferably in your own garden or back yard.

AS THE MOON GROWS
The moon, as the nearest heavenly body of the dark and mysterious night, has had many superstitions attached to it.

The waxing and waning of the moon appeared magical — and was believed to have been caused by supernatural forces.

One old superstition, which still exists, is that as the moon becomes fuller, it brings good luck. However, a completely full moon causes bad luck.

"HE'D DO MUCH BETTER
WITHOUT ALL THOSE
GOOD LUCK HORSESHOES!"

MODERN SCARAB

John F. Kennedy served as president for not quite 3 years before his unfortunate death on November 22, 1963. On March 24, 1964, the United States Mint issued 26 million Kennedy half dollars.

The new coins quickly became popular as charms and are still saved by some people. They are widely carried on key chains for good luck, a form of modern scarab (see photo on page 37).

The origins of this superstition are also lost. Legend has it that the Garden of Eden abounded in 4 leaf clovers and that Eve took one of them with her when she and Adam were expelled. This story undoubtedly was made up to explain a superstition that already existed. The 4 leaf clover's attraction probably lies in the fact that it is unusual and rare. In the superstitious ancient world, everything out of the ordinary had a special meaning.

Will the athlete win?

By the principle of sympathetic magic, any object can become lucky. Some people regard a coin they have found as a charm that will bring more good fortune. Many stores display as a charm the first dollar paid to them. Magically, more dollars are supposed to follow the first.

An athlete who has worn a particular article of clothing when he has been playing unusually well may come to regard it as lucky. Without it, he may refuse to play or at least feel very uncomfortable. One heavyweight boxing champion held up the start of a fight while he sent a trainer back to the hotel to pick up his lucky bathrobe. He would not enter the ring without it.

Athletes, actors, and gamblers seem to be particularly superstitious. These occupations contain a great deal of uncertainty. Can the athlete win? Does the audience like the actor? Will the gambler continue to lose? For such people, a lucky charm may really have a good effect. Having it on hand may help to relax their nervousness and allow them to play or perform better. But it would be really difficult to convince a truly superstitious person — athlete, actor, gambler, or anybody — that the luck in his charm was really all in his head.

MANY MAGIC POWERS
This cluster of purple amethyst crystals is shown here uncut and unpolished, as it comes from the earth. Amethyst is the birthstone of February and has been known since early times.

The Greeks and Romans believed that if a man wore an amethyst he could drink wine without becoming drunk. The amethyst was said to have many other magic powers, among them protecting soldiers, helping hunters, curing toothaches, and keeping away hail and locusts.

Birthstones

Some charms are general and are supposed to work for everybody. An actor and a carpenter, for example, might both believe in the good luck of a 4 leaf clover. Other charms, like birthstones, are supposed to bring luck to only one group of people. The origin of the birthstone superstition goes back to the magic theories of astrologers in the Middle Ages.

They believed that different stones had the power to bring good fortune at different times of the year. In order to be "in harmony" with the date, astrologers and their followers would change the stones they wore accordingly. Gradually this practice changed to wearing a stone that corresponded to the section of the zodiac (see page 15) in which an individual was born.

Most birthstones today do not follow the zodiac. Instead, one or more stones are identified with each month of the year. If you want to look up your birthstone, the chances are that you will consult a list that has been prepared by a jewelers' association. Such lists vary greatly, especially from country to country.

The ancient superstition about birthstones still lingers with us. It is kept alive mostly by jewelers, who are more involved with selling a birthstone ring or locket than they are with superstition. Many people who buy such jewelry select their birthstones rather than other stones. Even if they are not particularly superstitious, they sometimes feel that the charm "might bring me luck."

BIRD SUPERSTITIONS

Early people looked with wonder on the flight of birds. They often disappeared into the sky — the home of gods and spirits — and this added further mystery to their strange ability to fly. It is understandable that many superstitions developed about birds. For example:

The first robin seen in the spring (top left) brings good luck. Finding a robin's nest with eggs in it is also lucky. But a robin that flies into a house will cause bad luck unless it is released.

The crow (bottom left) is often considered to be a messenger of bad news. Thus a crow that caws near a house is announcing a disaster for the people inside.

A general feeling of misfortune superstitiously surrounds the crow. A pet crow, however, is said to protect its owner against evil forces.

The owl (right) is a bird of the night. Its weird, hooting cry is a signal to superstitious people that a calamity is coming.

Yet the owl is also regarded as being wise. Perhaps this myth developed because during the day the owl sleeps with its large eyes open, staring straight ahead as if lost in thought.

Birds often are credited with the ability to predict the future, as in this country rhyme:

*When the swallow's nest
is high, summer is dry;
When the swallow's nest
is low, you can safely
reap and sow.*

INVENTION
OF A SUPERSTITION

Howard Carter and Lord Carnarvon became world famous in 1922 for finding the tomb of the Pharaoh Tutankhamen. When Lord Carnarvon died some months later, the "Pharaoh's Curse" was blamed.

The curse was mysterious and awesome — and a fraud. It was invented by reporters who wanted to provide their readers with an exciting story that would continue to sell newspapers and magazines.

Like many members of the expedition, Howard Carter — the chief discoverer of the tomb — lived a normal life span. He died in 1939 at the age of 66.

It's jinxed!

Certain objects are supposed to bring good luck, but others have a reputation of being *jinxed* — that is, of bringing bad luck. The Hope diamond, one of the world's greatest gems, is supposed to bring misfortune to its owners. Today, this jinxed stone is on display in the Smithsonian Institution in Washington, D.C. Its reputation for bad luck does not keep thousands of visitors from flocking to see it every year.

Places as well as objects can be jinxed. For example, consider the story of the "Pharaoh's Curse." The rulers, or kings, of ancient Egypt were called pharaohs. In 1922, archaeologists (scientists who study ancient civilizations) made a spectacular discovery in Egypt. They uncovered the tomb of the Pharaoh Tutankhamen, an event that made headlines throughout the world.

44

Shortly after the tomb was opened, 3 people who had been connected with the expedition died. They all died of different causes, and their deaths were entirely natural. But the coincidence unleashed a flood of stories that the tomb had been cursed.

There was a tale that the inscription "Death to those who enter this tomb" was carved above the tomb door. This inscription never existed. Nor did those who believed in the curse ever bother to explain how dozens of others connected with the expedition lived long and successful lives after entering the tomb. The story of the "Pharaoh's Curse" was kept alive in newspapers and magazines for years. In the end, it proved to be one of the biggest hoaxes in the history of superstition.

ANCIENT SENTRY

Egyptian tombs are protected against intruders by Anubis, a god with the form of a jackal.

In the drawing above, Anubis has tied up 2 enemies to prevent them from interfering with the trip of a dead pharaoh to the next world.

A similar or worse fate supposedly awaits robbers who want to invade a tomb for its riches or archaeologists who want to find new truths about the past.

Such beliefs make Egyptian tombs an especially good subject for stories of the supernatural, which still appear in articles, works of fiction, and movies.

Chapter 4

THE MAGIC OF WORDS AND NUMBERS

Do you remember the story of Rumpelstiltskin? It is an old German folk tale about a wonder-working dwarf and a girl. In order to save her life, the girl must make gold out of straw. The dwarf agrees to do this for her, but in return she must give him her first-born child.

When the girl does give birth, she regrets the bargain. The only way she can keep her child is to guess the dwarf's name. One day, through a lucky accident, the girl learns that his name is Rumpelstiltskin. When the dwarf finds out that his name has been discovered, he flies into a rage and is never heard from again.

Power in a name

The tale probably goes back to very ancient times, when a man's name had great and terrible significance. It was

MAGIC IN A PLANT'S NAME

The phrase "Open, Sesame" was made famous in the story *Ali Baba and the 40 Thieves.* When these words were spoken, they opened a cave containing treasure.

Sesame was and still is an important plant in Asia. The seeds are used as food and a source of oil — both for nutrition and in religious ceremonies.

The importance of the sesame plant suggests why its name was thought to have magic powers.

"Open, Sesame"

as much a part of a man as his arm. Even among some of the primitive peoples in the modern world, a tribesman will not reveal his real name to strangers.

Many Australian aborigines, people who lead primitive lives, have 2 names: a name which they are called in everyday life and a sacred name, which is never spoken out loud. The aborigine fears that an enemy who learns his sacred name could gain magic power to harm him. The Rumpelstiltskin story is based on a belief similar to that of the aborigines. That is why the dwarf became so enraged when the girl learned his name. She had not merely guessed a riddle — she had gained magic power over him.

Let the dry land appear

The power of words is clearly shown in the biblical commandment, "Thou shalt not take the name of the Lord thy God in vain." This means that one should not speak the name of God without respect.

The beginning of the Bible further testifies to the power the ancient Jews found in words. According to the Old Testament, the world was created when God gave the commands that appear at the beginning of the Book of Genesis. Among the many poetic passages are these words: "And God said, Let the waters under the heaven be gathered together unto one place, and let the dry land appear: and it was so." The biblical world, thus, began with words.

When ghosts seemed real

Even before the Bible, words had a magic power connected with them. Many people still feel that power. For example, "Do not speak ill of the dead" is a common saying. It is considered impolite to say anything bad about a person who has died recently. However, the desire to be polite is not all that keeps critical tongues quiet.

Often a vague thought is also present that disrespect to the dead can bring punishment. These feelings go back to the days when ghosts seemed as real as one's family or friends. Most people then believed — as some still do

SECRET NAME
Ishi was the last survivor of the Yahi tribe of Indians in California. He left the wilderness and lived with white people from 1911 to 1916, when he died.

Although he made friends among the whites, he never told them his real name. Ishi in the Yahi language simply means *man*.

He feared that he would be harmed if anyone outside his family knew his name. Some modern Peruvian Indians have the same belief.

today — that harsh words about a dead person might cause his ghost to become angry and seek revenge.

Some sayings have completely lost their original superstitious meanings. "Speak of the Devil" we might say as a joke when someone we are talking about unexpectedly enters the room. At one time, the full saying, "Speak of the Devil and he will appear," was no joke. It was a warning against speaking the dread name for fear that the Devil himself would appear on the spot.

(continued on page 57)

POWER IN A PROMISE
Seated here between 2 companions, the Chinese god Kwan-Ti upheld justice, encouraged literature, and opposed war. He was also the god of oath-taking and represented the highest qualities of loyalty and brotherhood.

An oath is a promise to tell the truth or fulfill a pledge. In practically all societies, the words of an oath are considered to have great power. Thus if a person breaks an oath, he may feel that he will be punished even if nobody else knows about it.

the workshop

Are newspaper horoscopes accurate?

Millions of people read newspaper horoscopes (discussed on page 16). They hope to learn how the day will turn out or how they can make the day more favorable. Are these people receiving valuable information? Or are they being misled? Of course, you cannot answer for them. But you can find out for yourself whether newspaper horoscopes really apply to your life.

Each day for 2 weeks cut your horoscope out of a newspaper. Also cut out the horoscopes of any 2 other birth signs. The majority of newspapers carry horoscope columns. If you do not receive a newspaper at home that has a horoscope column, try the library. You will probably find a horoscope column in one of the newspapers they receive, and you can copy the horoscopes.

At the same time, keep a daily diary. List the important things you do and events that take place that affect your life. Remember to include unusual happenings, strong feelings, significant discoveries, and the like.

After 2 weeks, compare your diary with the daily horoscopes. Did they forecast what happened to you most of the time? Half of the time? Hardly ever?

Is the language of the horoscopes so vague that many interpretations are possible? Or is the language specific enough to provide you with real information? One way to answer these questions is to check your diary against the 2 other horoscopes. Determine if their predictions were better, worse, or about the same.

Vague language is a magnet for those who would rather believe than question. It allows them to satisfy their desires and fears without the hard work that is usually necessary in solving problems. As an example of the difference between vague and specific language, consider the following 3 statements:

1. You will have a problem today. (Statement 1 does not tell us much because everybody has a few problems during the day.)

2. You will have a school problem today that requires a decision. (Statement 2 is more specific, but the information it provides is still vague. For example, many problems call for a decision. And a "school problem" can be anything — a lost ballpoint pen, failure in an examination, lateness, and so on.)

3. You will have an important school problem this afternoon because you will have to decide if you have enough spare time to join both the track team and the science club. (Statement 3 is specific because it describes the nature of the problem.)

Suppose you had read statement 1 and believed that it applied to the problem of the track team and the science club. You would have fallen for one of the oldest tricks in fortune telling — providing missing information that makes the fortune seem accurate.

Accuracy is not easy to measure when we are dealing with language. However, the 3 statements can serve as a rough — yet somewhat accurate — guide to the difference between vague and specific language. Compare the horoscopes with these statements. Is the language of the horoscopes closest to statement 1, 2, or 3? Do you conclude that newspaper horoscopes are vague or specific?

Take a giant to lunch

Astrology is a serious business for those who believe in it. Even believers, however, can enjoy a spark of humor to light up their solemn thoughts. As an exercise in humorous imagination, try writing some funny horoscopes. The samples that follow are reprinted with permission of Price/Stern/Sloan Publishers, Inc., from *You Were Born On A Rotten Day*, copyright 1969 by Jim Critchfield and Jerry Hopkins.

Kitchen activity is highlighted. Butter up a friend.

If you were born before 3:00 P.M. today, go home. You're too young to be working.

Make every effort to get to the heart of the matter. Take somebody's pulse tonight.

You are restless now and desirous of change. Try two dimes and a nickel.

If you are under three feet tall, avoid four-foot snowdrifts for a while.

Good day to have a bad day.

Good time for colossal undertaking. Take a giant to lunch.

What did you see?

Information that is passed from one person to another often goes through several changes. Such changes seem to take place frequently if an event is described that appears to be supernatural. For example, a man tells a friend, "I saw a light in the cemetery at 9:00 o'clock last night." The 5th or 6th person to pass this information along may well say, "Somebody saw a ghost in the cemetery last night at midnight."

The reason that the first link in a chain of information differs from the last link rarely involves dishonesty. Some people react with strong emotions to what they see or hear. Their observations tend to be altered by their own fears, likes, dislikes, hopes, and general views of life. Also most of us do not have highly accurate memories, and we forget or change some details that we observe.

Here is one way to test how information is changed when it is passed from person to person. Ask a friend to study the ghost picture for 30 seconds. Time him with a watch that has a second hand. Then take the book away, and ask him to draw the picture from memory. He can take all the time he wants to make the drawing. Repeat the process with at least 5 friends. The drawing in the book should be seen only by the first friend. Each of the others should study the drawing made by the previous person.

The final drawing probably will vary greatly from the original. On page 56, you can see the final drawing of a test made for this book with 8 people. Such tests lead to an important conclusion that applies to most research:

Information may change if it is passed from person to person. When you do research, it is desirable — and often necessary — to start with original material that has had the least possible chance of being changed.

Superstitions of young children

The human mind is reluctant to leave a mystery unsolved. A gap in our knowledge, a happening that we do not understand, an event that does not fit into the order of things — all these tend to make us dissatisfied until we have found an explanation.

Today we attempt to explain the unknown scientifically. But before the methods and tools of science were widespread, how could man explain the wind, or static electricity, or an eclipse. For the most part, he created explanations that we now call superstitions.

Young children sometimes explain the world in a similar way — that is, they create superstitions. The psychologist Jean Piaget described 9 explanations that are used by young children to show what causes natural events to take place.

Read these explanations, which follow. Then ask a 4- or 5-year-old child (a group would be even better) questions based on what you have read. For example: Why does the wind blow? What makes shadows? Why is it cloudy?

You will find that his answers — the causes he supplies to explain natural events — closely resemble some of the superstitions discussed in this book.

1. The natural event has a will of its own. The wind blows because it wants to.

2. The natural event has a purpose. The wind blows to make us cool. In the picture, the wind had a different purpose — to move an early Finnish sailing ship. The 3 knots in the rope were tied by a sorcerer. Each knot was supposed to control a wind of different strength. If the ship was becalmed, the sailors hoped to release a helpful wind by untying a magic knot.

3. The closeness of 2 or more things makes them act together. Rain falls because there is thunder. The wind blows because trees move.

4. One thing is part of another. Trees have shadows; that is why objects on a table also have shadows.

5. Magic — the thoughts and gestures of people can influence natural events. It is cloudy outside because my father is angry.

6. Moral — natural events take place because it is only right that they do so. It rains because it ought to rain.

7. God or godlike beings cause natural events to occur. The clouds move across the sky because God is pushing them.

8. Natural events and objects have characteristics that are lifelike. The leaf falls because it grew tired of holding on. The sun shines because it is happy.

9. Natural events and objects have forces in them — or are acted on by forces — that are not human or otherwise alive. At this point the child looks at the world more logically. He begins to understand that a moving object, like the sun, does not have to be alive.

Heroic men who fought the witch superstition

All men were not silent about the cruel madness of the witchcraft belief. Here and there a courageous voice was heard strongly attacking the mistreatment of innocent people accused of being witches (see picture). It was dangerous for these men to speak out against the witchcraft belief because they could have been persecuted for helping the Devil.

A few heroic opponents of the cruelty of witch trials are discussed here. Why is it worth thinking about what they did and said a few hundred years ago? Perhaps because it is rewarding to discover that when we see the worst in human nature, we also can find the best.

You may want to do further research into the lives of these men who opposed cruelty being practiced in the name of religion. A rewarding place to start is *The Encyclopedia of Witchcraft and Demonology*, by Rossell Hope Robbins, from which the following examples were taken.

Herman Loher was a court official in a German town when a special witch judge arrived and started holding trials. Loher criticized the trials and, with his life in jeopardy, escaped to Holland. In a book published in 1676, he said that being tried for witchcraft "is just as if a condemned person were forced to fight with lions, bears, and wolves for his life, and were prevented from protecting himself, since he is deprived of weapons of every description."

Johann Meyfarth, a professor of religion, lived in the early 17th century in Germany. He had personally witnessed many witchcraft trials and tortures. Attacking the witchcraft hunters in language that all could understand, he wrote: "Listen, you money-hungering judges and blood-thirsty prosecutors, the apparitions [appearances] of the Devil are all lies."

John Holt (1642-1710) has a place in history for his support of civil and religious liberties. As Chief Justice of England, he did much to eliminate the witchcraft hysteria. Holt became celebrated in his day for instructing juries to free accused witches. His opinions influenced many lower courts to follow the same practice.

Friedrich von Spee (1591-1635), a German priest, voiced a powerful protest against the cruel punishment of witches. He boldly attacked those who accused and tried witches, saying: "They made it their business to prove guilt, holding it a disgrace if any were acquitted. For this work they were well paid. . . ."

Alonzo Salazar de Frias was a Spanish *inquisitor*, an investigator of witches. Dissatisfied with the evidence of witchcraft offered by other inquisitors, he interviewed some 1,800 supposed witches. His conclusion was startling: "I have not found even indications from which to infer that a single act of witchcraft has really occurred. . . ." Salazar drew up a set of instructions for investigating witchcraft that was adopted in Spain in 1614. With just a few exceptions, witchcraft trials in Spain disappeared forever.

What if?

How different would your life be from what it is now if you were deeply superstitious? In this workshop project, you can learn something about the thoughts and actions of a person to whom superstitions are very real.

Start by writing an account of everything that happens to you during a day. Your story can be as long as you like but should not be shorter than 2 or 3 pages. Now, from the superstitions that follow, pick 10 that you find particularly interesting.

Rewrite your account of the day's happenings, weaving the 10 superstitions into the story. As you write, imagine

that your understanding of the world and your actions are guided by these superstitious beliefs. What if you were convinced that:

Big feet are a sign of intelligence.

It is unlucky to throw away a piece of bread.

Bragging about money or accomplishments invites bad luck.

A dream that occurs in a strange bed will come true.

A cat washing its face means that a visitor is coming.

Crossed fingers make a wish come true.

Cutting bread at both ends of the loaf is bad luck.

To fall means bad luck, which can be overcome by kicking the object that caused the fall.

"Pick up a pin, pick up sorrow." But some disagree: "See a pin, let it lie, all the day you'll have to cry."

Leaning a broom against a bed is unlucky.

Sweeping dust out of the front door means sweeping out the family's good fortune.

It is good luck to have a first or last name with 7 letters.

Seeing one's shadow by moonlight is bad luck.

It is good luck to see a shooting star.

A person who enters a house with his left foot first will have bad luck.

It is good luck to sing while bathing.

Killing a spider brings poverty or rain.

A "lucky penny" should be kept and never spent.

Demons cannot enter a house if a jar of water with a knife in it is placed behind a door.

It is good luck accidentally to put on a garment wrong, providing it is kept that way for the whole day.

A cricket that comes into a house brings good luck with it.

Stomachache can be cured by tying a string around an ankle.

Cutting fingernails on Friday or Sunday brings bad luck.

Sneezing 3 times brings good luck.

Sleeping with books under the pillow helps in passing an examination.

Company is coming if a knife, fork, or spoon is dropped.

If somebody enters a house by one door and leaves by another, he will have bad luck.

If the bottom of a person's foot itches, he will be walking in strange places.

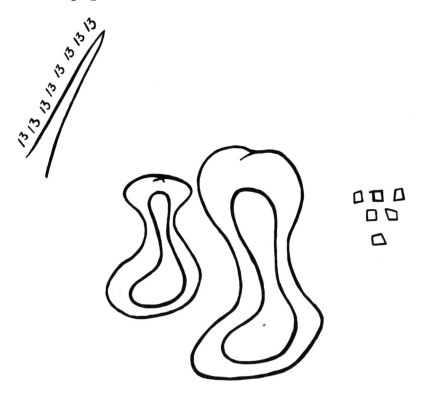

This is the 8th drawing made from the original on page 51.

(continued from page 48)

The indignant ghost

Often we hesitate even to speak the name of a dead person. At a funeral, mourners will talk about "the deceased" or "the departed." If we do speak the name of the dead person, it is generally in a low voice. Not to do so would be considered bad manners by most people. But once men feared that a name spoken out loud was so powerful that it would call up the ghost.

Sir James Frazer, one of the pioneers in the study of superstition, discovered a similar belief among the tribesmen of Central Australia. These people are afraid to utter the name of a dead person during the period of mourning. If the name is mentioned, it is in a whisper "for fear of disturbing and annoying the man's spirit which is walking about in ghostly form. If the ghost hears his name, he concludes that his kinfolk are not mourning for him properly; if their grief were genuine, they could not bear to bandy his name about. Touched to the quick by their hard-hearted indifference, the indignant ghost will come and trouble them in dreams."

Who is talking about you?

Words have such power that even at a distance they can make your ears burn — so goes the popular superstition. If the burning is in the right ear, all well and good, for you are being praised. But if the burning is in the left ear, watch out: Someone is speaking badly of you.

Ringing in the ear also is supposed to mean that you are being talked about. How can you find out who is

WORDS TO THE STARS
What better place to address magic words than the distant and mysterious stars. Jiminy Cricket, in the film *Pinocchio*, sings "When You Wish Upon A Star." Another and older appeal to the stars goes:

> *Star light, star bright,*
> *first star I see tonight*
> *I wish I may,*
> *   I wish I might*
> *have the wish I wish*
> *   tonight.*

©Walt Disney Productions

WHAMMY!

This baseball trainer is putting a double whammy on the other team. A *whammy* is a spell intended to defeat an opponent. Sports superstitions are widespread. For example:

Radio and television announcers never mention a baseball no-hitter while it is in progress. If a hit spoils the no-hitter, superstitious fans will blame the announcer for breaking the magic rule of silence.

RINGING EARS
AND SPIDER WEBS

Are your ears ringing? Did you see a spider spinning a web? Superstitious people say that both are signs that somebody is gossiping about you. Here is an old New England remedy: Pinch your left ear, and it will make him bite his tongue.

doing the talking? It is easy, according to one superstition. Just repeat the names of the people that you know, and right after the name of the talker the ringing will stop. Whether it is better to have your left or right ear ring depends on the superstition. Some people believe that a ringing in the right ear means praise, and a ringing in the left ear means criticism. But others believe that the opposite is true.

Gamblers' magic words

When you play or watch a team sport like baseball, it makes sense to shout encouragement to your team. But it is useless to shout encouragement to a deck of cards. Yet we often do that very thing during a card game. We hope that our words will somehow influence the placement of the cards in the deck. Dice players have a whole set of hopeful expressions they shout during a game. The most familiar is "7 come 11."

58

In a game of chance, like cards or dice, a player has no control over the outcome. Do gamblers, then, really believe that their words will influence the turn of the cards or the fall of the dice? Most would say no, when questioned in a calm moment. But in the excitement of a game, these same gamblers often fall back on a primitive method of attempting to establish control — shouting magic words.

Although words will not change the outcome of a game, they may help the gambler in another way. By shouting, he "lets off steam" and relieves the anxieties caused by not knowing whether he is going to win or lose.

When all is quiet

Silence also has superstitions attached to it. You might be sitting in a roomful of people, all talking noisily to one another. Suddenly all conversation seems to pause at once, and the room is quiet. When this sort of silence occurs, people often become uncomfortable. Someone may say, "It must be 20 minutes after the hour."

There is a popular American superstition that silence occurs at 20 minutes after the hour, honoring Abraham Lincoln, who supposedly died at 8:20. As a matter of fact, Lincoln was shot in the evening of April 14, 1865 and died at 7:22 the next morning.

Silence has always been associated with death. At funerals, the mourners are asked to observe a few moments of silence out of respect for the person who died. Another interpretation of sudden silence in a room is that someone present is fated to die within the year. A more cheerful superstition is that talk has stopped because an angel is passing through the room.

Lucky and unlucky numbers

Like language, mathematics is a marvelous invention that is useful in almost every human activity. We can therefore see why numbers, along with words, developed many superstitious associations. In chapter 1, we discussed some superstitions that surround the numbers 13 and 7. Let us look at a few other number superstitions.

DISAPPEARING

A 2-dollar bill is considered unlucky. On August 10, 1966, the Treasury Department announced that it would no longer print 2-dollar bills because of "a limited public interest." However, a small number of these bills are still in circulation, and the superstition about them continues.

GAME ONCE CONSIDERED TO BE MAGIC

Magic squares were worn as charms in ancient times in China and India. It was thought then that the numbers themselves had magic powers. Today we regard magic squares as games or interesting exercises in mathematics.

Each row, each column, and each of the 2 diagonals in a magic square add up to the same number. In the square below, the number is 34. This square permits some other remarkable additions:

The 4 center squares. The 4 corner squares. The 4 corner sets of squares (for example, 16, 3, 5, 10). The 4 sets of slanting squares (for example, 5, 3, 14, 12).

16	3	2	13
5	10	11	8
9	6	7	12
4	15	14	1

To start with, many people have personal lucky and unlucky numbers. If you have to choose a number for some purpose, should it be odd or even? Superstitious people will tell you that odd numbers are luckier than even numbers. Do you believe that a 2-dollar bill is unlucky? Two-dollar bills are now rare, but the expression "unlucky as a 2-dollar bill" is still heard. This superstition probably started in card and dice playing, where 2 is the lowest number and thus unlucky.

Some people consider 3 to be a lucky number. Yet lighting 3 candles or 3 cigarettes on 1 match is regarded as unlucky. How about 5? One lucky sign, seen everywhere — for example, on Christmas trees; on the flags of many nations, including the United States and the Soviet Union; and on trademarks of businesses — is the 5-pointed star. The favorable feeling connected with 5 dates back more than 2,500 years to the Greeks. They used 5 as perhaps their most important symbol (sign): it stood for the world.

Numerology

Ancient mathematicians developed magic theories about the ways in which numbers related to human events. As mathematics advanced over several hundred years, mathematicians abandoned their beliefs in the magic of numbers. However, such beliefs have not disappeared. Some of them still can be found in *numerology*, the study of how numbers are supposed to influence human life.

Few people today follow the superstitious study of numerology. But sometimes one of the numerologists' superstitious ideas becomes widely known. As we have said, when a terrible event takes place, people try to make sense of it. In an attempt to do so, they often turn to superstitions, like numerology, for an answer. It is hard to accept the fact that chance or an accident can deeply change our lives. That is why, perhaps, numerologists found an audience when they attempted to explain the assassination of President John F. Kennedy on November 22, 1963.

Is it just coincidence?

A large number of superstitions, numerological and otherwise, surround the death of President Kennedy. One of the most persistent superstitions is that his death is linked to the death of President Lincoln. Numerologists point out that the names of both murdered presidents, Kennedy and Lincoln, contain 7 letters. And as we have seen, 7 is regarded as a magic number.

The names of Kennedy's accused assassin and Lincoln's assassin, numerologists also say, have 15 letters. If we count up the letters in Lee Harvey Oswald (President Kennedy's accused assassin) and in John Wilkes Booth (President Lincoln's assassin), we see that they are right. Numerologists ask, Is it just coincidence that the numbers 7 and 15 appear twice? When we look at the way these numbers were selected, we can clearly see that the answer to the question is yes.

STAGE FOR SUPERSTITION

Numerologists sometimes relate number theories to great natural events. For example, an eclipse of the sun provides a dramatic stage on which to present the start or finish of a prediction.

Such practices are not limited to numerology. Throughout history, eclipses have encouraged superstitious thinking, as in the military expedition of Athens against Syracuse in 415 B.C.

Nikias, commander of the Athenians, was at the point of retreating when an eclipse of the moon occurred. He chose to regard this as a bad omen for the enemy and predicted their defeat. He delayed his retreat, losing both his army and his life.

SCIENTIFIC METHOD REQUIRES DUPLICATION

An important principle of the scientific method is that the same test can be applied everywhere. Thus a laboratory in Buenos Aires can obtain the same test results as a laboratory in Cleveland.

Numerologists, however, do not follow this principle. Their results usually apply to a single problem that they select. When these results are tested elsewhere on similar problems, they tend to fall apart.

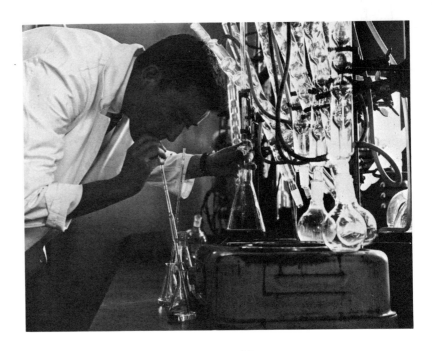

The same test for everything

In order to have the numbers work out to their satisfaction, the numerologists make up rules as they go along. They search for letter combinations that will fit their magic number theories and ignore letter combinations that are not suitable. This approach may seem dishonest, but most numerologists are not trying to cheat. They just do not follow one of the chief rules of modern scientific investigation — apply the same test to everything.

For example, they select only the last names of the presidents to obtain 7 letters. Then they select the full names of Lee Harvey Oswald and John Wilkes Booth to obtain 15 letters. To start with, this approach — last names in one instance, full names in the other — does not sound too convincing.

But let us go one step further and apply the same test to everything. We begin by selecting the last names of Oswald and Booth. As we can quickly see, there are 6 letters in Oswald and 5 letters in Booth. Continuing the test, we now count up the letters in the full names of the presidents. John Fitzgerald Kennedy has 21 letters, and Abraham Lincoln has 14 letters. At this point, we need go no further. We can see that the tragic deaths of both presidents are not in any way explainable by numerology.

The "fatal 20" presidents

One of the best known number superstitions in America also concerns the deaths of presidents. This is the "fatal 20" superstition, which holds that presidents elected at 20-year intervals will die in office. The starting point for this supposed cycle is the election of 1840. A *cycle* is a series of events that continue to happen in the same order.

William H. Harrison, elected president in 1840, died in office. Twenty years afterward, in 1860, Abraham Lincoln was elected and later assassinated. James A. Garfield, elected in 1880, was also assassinated. So was William McKinley, elected in 1900. The next president to die in this cycle was Warren G. Harding. Elected in 1920, he died in office. Then Franklin D. Roosevelt, elected in 1940, died in office. And, of course, John F. Kennedy, elected in 1960, was assassinated.

Only two presidents elected in the 20-year cycle lived out their terms. Both were elected before 1840: Thomas Jefferson in 1800 and James Monroe in 1820.

Long before the election of 1960, the fatal 20 superstition was widely believed. Some people predicted a tragic end for the president elected in that year. When John F. Kennedy was elected and then assassinated, it appeared that the curse of fatal 20 had struck again.

Unusual but not supernatural

The 20-year cycle seems to work. Or does it? We can find the answer by seeing if all the presidents involved fit into the cycle in the same way. Let us start with Abraham Lincoln, who was first elected in 1860 and then reelected in 1864. He was assassinated after his reelection. William McKinley was elected in 1896 and again in 1900. He, too, was assassinated after his reelection.

President Lincoln possibly can be fitted into the 20-year cycle on the basis of his first term (1860). But President McKinley can get in only on his second term (1900). These deaths do not match each other nor do they match the deaths of the other presidents.

President Franklin D. Roosevelt is even more of a problem for numerologists. He was first elected in 1932 and does not fit into the 20-year cycle until his third term,

DEFIED SUPERSTITION
The only president to die in office who was not elected during the "fatal 20" cycle was Zachary Taylor. He was elected in 1848 and died in 1850.

63

COINCIDENCE

Numerologists find it easiest to impress people who do not know much about mathematics. As the numerologist juggles his numbers, he creates an atmosphere of mystery in which the numbers seem to have a purpose of their own.

Yet mathematics is a science. Its mysteries come from lack of knowledge, not the supernatural. For example, people often are startled when a number repeats itself frequently.

Such coincidences are far more common in mathematics than is usually supposed. A good illustration is the famous "birthday coincidence."

Consider a large crowd, like the one in the photograph. Imagine that the crowd is divided into groups of 24. What are the chances that 2 people in each group were born on the same month and day?

Since there are 365 possible birthdays in a year, the chances may seem slim. However, the opposite is true.

The chances are a little better than 50 percent that 2 people in each group have the same birthday. This means that in slightly more than half the groups, 2 people out of the 24 that make up a group were born on the same day and month.

Number coincidences like this may seem startling — but they are not mysterious. They can be clearly proven by anyone who knows the laws of probability.

in 1940. To make the cycle work, the numerologists again had to change the rules.

Mathematicians have applied logic (sound reasoning) to studying the deaths of the 7 presidents we have discussed. Their figures show that the chances for the 7 deaths occurring are about 1 in 100. We can conclude that the series of deaths are unusual but not miraculous or supernatural. The president elected in 1980 need not worry about the 20-year cycle.

Measuring the Great Pyramid

Famous monuments, like famous events, often have number superstitions attached to them. So many numerological theories centered on the Great Pyramid of Egypt that a pseudoscience of *pyramidology* developed. A *pseudoscience* is an activity that appears to be scientific but is not. Pyramidology was popular a century ago and still has followers today.

The pyramidologist believes that the Great Pyramid was not just the tomb of an ancient Egyptian pharaoh but really a vast mathematical puzzle. By interpreting the measurements of the Great Pyramid, the pyramidologists have attempted to show that a great deal of the world's knowledge lies within this structure.

What can a pyramidologist accomplish with numbers? Possibly he may discover some relationships that are true. Or he may create some that exist only in his mind. For example, when the height of the Great Pyramid (481 feet) is multiplied by 1 billion, the answer is approximately the distance from the earth to the sun. If you enjoy mathematics, you can work out similar number games. You can easily create a relationship between the height of any tall building and the distance from the earth to the moon. But what would such numbers mean? Would any scientific truths be revealed?

Pyramidologists find not only scientific truths but the key to the future in the measurements of the Great Pyramid. By interpreting these measurements, pyramidologists claim they can determine the dates for the creation of the world, the biblical flood, and even the date on which the world will end. Many of these interpretations were made during the last century. At that time, pyramidologists declared that the world would end in 1911. Modern pyramidologists have been forced to revise that date.

The "fiveness" of the Great Pyramid

Pyramidologists say that 5 is the key number in the Great Pyramid. "This intense fiveness could not have been accidental," one wrote. To the pyramidologist, the fives are related in some way to the 5 senses, the 5 fingers and toes, the 5 books of Moses, and so on.

SUPERNATURAL SCENE?

How many groups of 3 can you find in the park? For example, there are 3 dogs and 3 birds in flight. If you count more than 6 groups of 3, you have a good eye.

In looking at this scene, a numerologist might give the number 3 a supernatural meaning because, in his opinion, it appears often.

Here he would part company with the mathematician, who would interpret the park scene with the laws of probability.

Let us assume that both men are sincere. One explains what he sees by referring to supernatural causes. The other applies the scientific method. Which approach would you use?

But are these vague relationships between the fives of the Great Pyramid and other fives really meaningful? No, they are not. Martin Gardner's book *Fads & Fallacies* (published by Dover) shows how easy it is to make up number relationships.

"Just for fun, if one looks up the facts about the Washington Monument in the *World Almanac*, he will find considerable fiveness. Its height is 555 feet and 5 inches. The base is 55 feet square, and the windows are set at 500 feet from the base. If the base is multiplied by 60 (or 5 times the number of months in a year) it gives 3,300, which is the weight of the capstone in pounds. Also the word *Washington* has exactly 10 letters (2×5). And if the weight of the capstone is multiplied by the base, the result is 181,500 — a fairly close approximation of the speed of light in miles per second."

Mr. Gardner's numbers are fun to play with, but numerologists are serious about their work. There is, in a way, a sadness about their seriousness, for much of what they do is useless. As we have seen, numerologists usually select only those numbers that will fit into their theories — an approach that allows them to prove just about anything. Most people, therefore, regard numerology as a collection of superstitions, nothing more.

Chapter 5

WITCHCRAFT — SUPERSTITION RUN WILD

In folklore and fairy stories, a witch is usually pictured as an old woman who lives deep in the forest and possesses evil powers. Is this the only type of witch? Not at all — tribes in every part of the world had (and many still have) *witch doctors*, sometimes called *medicine men, shamans,* or *sorcerers*. Their duties, depending on the tribe and its customs, may include healing the sick, making predictions, speaking with spirits, finding the best hunting areas, and causing rain to fall.

WHAT DOES A WITCH LOOK LIKE? The answer varies with the imagination of the person who is asking the question. Many pictures of witches, however, have 1 feature in common — powerful eyes that are supposed to help in casting a spell. According to superstitious belief, men, too, can be witches.

3 WEIRD SISTERS

Shakespeare's tragic play *Macbeth* took place in 11th century Scotland. Today we usually regard the 3 "weird sisters" of the play as witches. Actually they were sorcerers.

The difference is that witches were people who made a pact with the Devil, a practice that supposedly began 5 centuries later.

As late as the middle of the 19th century, fires were burned on remote Scottish hilltops to keep away witches who might steal infants, ruin crops, or kill farm animals.

In a broad sense, a witch was the same as a magician. Like an ancient magician, a witch engaged in supernatural activities — for example, she supposedly told fortunes, made magic charms, and controlled future events. (The magician of today, who amazes us on a stage, does not claim any supernatural powers. He openly admits that his "magic" is really a series of clever tricks.)

The Devil's plot

Witches in Europe came to be generally accepted as part of the society in which they lived. An English warrior in the year A.D. 500 might consult a witch to learn the outcome of a future battle. An Italian witch in A.D. 1300 might provide a charm against the fever. However, in Europe during the 16th and 17th centuries, the word *witch* took on a new and terrifying meaning.

A witch was declared to be someone who had made a pact (agreement) with the Devil. A man could be a witch, but most accused of witchcraft were women. What made a witch dangerous was that she had sided with the forces of the Devil against God. Witchcraft itself was regarded as a religion of evil. According to their accusers, witches were part of the Devil's vast plot to overthrow God and the Christian religion on earth.

Uncontrolled feelings

After witchcraft became a religious matter, the public's attitude toward witches changed. From acceptance, it turned into doubt and then into *hysteria*. In this mental state, people behave with uncontrolled feelings, especially fear. Why did this great change in attitude occur? Of the many reasons, 2 stand out — power and greed.

Political and religious leaders whipped up the hysteria to protect their own positions. The charge of witchcraft became a weapon. People who held different political or religious views could be accused of witchcraft and executed. Envy also frequently guided the finger that pointed at an accused witch. "It was malice and jealousy," wrote the historian George L. Burr, "which oftenest dictated the names denounced in the torture chamber. Wealth, learning, beauty, goodness — these were often the very conditions of accusation."

The persecution of witches was greatest where a witch's property could be taken away. The rules for sharing in this piracy depended on the country or the locality. Thus the property might be kept or shared by the king, his aides, church officials, the local lord, and town officials. Often the person who accused the witch was also given a share. In a few places, like England, laws did not permit a witch's property to be seized. Where such laws existed, witch hunting was not as cruel or as widespread.

The need for proof

At first, many of the common people were not too concerned with the witchcraft accusations. But after years of propaganda about the dangers of witchcraft, even the doubters were often won over. Those few who had the courage to denounce the witch hunters often found themselves accused of witchcraft. Many were either killed or forced from then on to remain silent.

The witchcraft hysteria is probably history's worst example of superstition run wild. It is a chilling lesson of what can happen to people when they completely abandon the need for proof before believing in something.

To primitive tribesmen, a magician could be either good or evil. To men of the 16th and 17th centuries, a witch

EXCHANGE
A witch and the Devil are shown here going through the ceremony of signing a pact. In exchange for money and power, the witch supposedly agreed to such things as:
- Denying the Christian religion.
- Swearing allegiance to the Devil.
- Surrendering her soul to the Devil.
- Keeping silent about her dealings with the Devil.

THE DEVIL COLLECTS
According to legend, when a witch made a pact with the Devil, she had to keep her part of the bargain. This German picture, over 400 years old, shows the Devil taking away a child that had been promised to him.

could only be evil. One witch hunter was quite surprised to find that not everyone believed that storms and other natural disasters were caused by witchcraft.

What about good witches?

Witches were often accused of raising storms, making people ill, or ruining crops. However, a witch did not have to be convicted of such acts in order to be condemned to death. The crime was not what the witch did but the fact that she was supposed to have made a pact with the Devil.

What if a witch was considered by everybody to be a good person? It did not matter, as we can see in this statement by William Perkins, a late 16th century religious thinker:

"Though the witch were in many respects profitable [helpful to others], and did not hurt but procured much good, yet, because he hath renounced God as his king and governor and hath bound himself by other laws to the service of the enemies of God and his church, death is his portion justly assigned to him by God: He may not live."

Could a witch defend herself?

Accused witches who said they were innocent were tortured to obtain confessions that they had dealt with the Devil. Even those who confessed immediately for

STORM COMING
Many accused witches confessed under torture that they could control the weather. In this picture from 1489, witches are shown creating a storm.

TRIAL BY WATER
One method of trying a witch was to tie her with a rope and drop her into water. If she floated, she was being helped by evil magic and was guilty. If she sank, she was innocent — but might drown.

WITCH BURNING
Convicted witches were almost always burned. Sometimes, as an act of mercy, the witch was killed first.

The burning of witches was approved in the teachings of some of the great Christian philosophers, such as:

Augustine (A.D. 354-430), Thomas Aquinas (about 1227-1274), and John Calvin (1509-1564).

fear of torture could not escape this cruel treatment. They, too, were tortured to make certain they were not confessing falsely. For a confession to be considered acceptable, it had to be obtained under torture. If a confession was taken back, it did not matter — all confessions were considered permanent.

Under such conditions, how could accused witches defend themselves? The answer is that none could. There was practically no escape for an accused witch. As a result, some 200,000 innocent people in Europe were tortured and executed. The famous Salem witchcraft trials, though shameful enough, were mild when compared with what had taken place in Europe. During these trials, in colonial Massachusetts in the early 1690's, fewer than 20 people were executed.

It seems hard to believe today, but not all of the witch hunters had evil or dishonest intentions. Some really believed that by torture they would be able to save a witch's soul, even though they might destroy her body. They thought it was their duty to protect the world from the unseen evil forces that threatened it. That is why people who persecute others in the belief that they are uncovering a secret plot are still called *witch hunters*.

The trial of the Templars

An early example of how the witchcraft hysteria was created can be seen in the unhappy fate of the Knights Templars. This military-religious group had been founded

ATTACKING A PEASANT
The witch, in this late 15th century illustration, seeks to gain power over the peasant. She has shot him in the foot with a magic arrow. His foot has started to swell, and he has removed his shoe. The swelling will disappear if he agrees to obey the witch.

71

in the year 1118 to fight in the Crusades. They continued to exist after the Crusades and grew rich.

King Philip IV of France coveted the wealth of the Templars. Technically, the charge brought against them in 1307 was *heresy* — holding religious opinions opposed to those of the recognized church. The charge could just as easily have been witchcraft, but the word had not yet come into favor. The king was supported by many churchmen who feared and disliked the religious ideas of the Templars.

The specific heresies they were charged with — worshiping the Devil, denying God, and engaging in wicked practices — were typical of later witchcraft trials. The methods of conducting the trial were also typical. The accused were tortured until they confessed to whatever it was that the torturers wanted to hear. The leader of the Templars was burned as a heretic in 1314, despite a courageous speech in which he withdrew his confession. The once powerful group was destroyed.

The witches' sabbat

As the witchcraft hysteria grew, the investigators began to make up certain practices that witches were supposed to follow. They said, for example, that all witches regularly attended a *sabbat* — a great gathering of witches and demons to honor the Devil. A *demon* is an evil spirit, generally considered to be an ally of the Devil.

An informer might say that he had seen a woman at a sabbat. This kind of accusation was almost as good as a conviction. There was no way for the accused witch to prove she had not attended the sabbat. Even if she had witnesses testify that she had been asleep in her bed the night of the sabbat, she would not be found innocent. The prosecutors would answer that the Devil, disguised as the accused witch, had taken her place in bed that night while she was attending the sabbat.

How Halloween began

In modern customs surrounding Halloween, Christian and pagan traditions are all mixed in with stories of the witches' sabbat. For Roman Catholics, November 1 is All

HORNED DEVIL
This sculpture from the Middle Ages is still standing on a church in Paris. It represents Baphomet, a horned devil with wings whom the Templars were accused of worshiping.

WHAT WAS A SABBAT LIKE?
Imaginations ran wild in picturing a witches' sabbat. In this painting by the Spanish artist Francisco de Goya (1746-1828), the Devil appears as a great goat.

One hysterical account — written by a man who was a judge at witchcraft trials — set a record for the number of witches present at a sabbat:

"The sabbat resembles a fair of merchants, mingling together, angry and half crazed, arriving from all quarters, a surging crowd of some one hundred thousand devotees of Satan."

UNLUCKY TO SOME, BEAUTIFUL TO OTHERS
A witch's familiar often was thought to be a cat, especially if it was black. Superstitions still cling to black cats. For example:

It is bad luck to see a black cat — worse luck if it crosses one's path. Black cats can cause misery, disease, even death. They are ghosts, demons, or other unfriendly spirits.

Of course, cats are neither lucky nor unlucky. Many cat lovers prize black cats because often they are beautiful animals.

Saints' Day — dedicated to all saints and martyrs, known and unknown.

An old name for the day is Hallowmas. *Hallow* means holy. *Eve* means the evening before a special day or holiday; therefore, the night before Hallowmas is Hallowmas Eve, or *E'en*.

In some parts of the world, pagan festivals marking the beginning of winter fell at about the same time as All Saints' Day. Some of these festivals involved telling ghost stories and dressing up in costumes. The ghost stories and the stories of the witches' sabbat were often combined and later could not be told apart.

Today, many people believe that Halloween has an ancient and special meaning in the history of witchcraft. But this is not so. Witchcraft and Halloween were not associated until long after the witchcraft hysteria had died down.

Unlucky black cats

Witchcraft investigators claimed that each witch had a demon as a companion and adviser. The name for such a demon was a *familiar spirit* or simply a *familiar*. Supposedly, familiars took the form of small animals — most often a cat. Many of our superstitions about unlucky black cats (see photograph) come from their association with witchcraft.

If the accused witch did not happen to have a cat, the investigators would assert that a dog, chicken, goose,

SPIRIT SENTRY
Today jack o'lanterns are cheerful decorations for Halloween. But once they had a protective purpose — to frighten away evil spirits on Halloween night.

rat, mouse, even a fly was her familiar. Such accusations were easily proven since every house was bound to have at least some sort of small animal or insect in it. If a fly was seen buzzing about an accused witch during the trial, her accusers would say that it was the familiar trying to aid its mistress.

The identification of cats with witchcraft was disastrous during times of plague. Many people thought that cats, being representatives of the Devil, were responsible for the plague. In fact, rats carry plague germs. During an epidemic, cats were often slaughtered in great numbers. By killing all cats, the rats' most effective natural enemy, superstitious people actually helped to spread the disease.

Were there real witches?

Or was the fear of witchcraft based on nothing? A few scholars believe that there really was a kind of underground (secret organization) of witches. They think that a witch cult, or group, existed that worshiped an ancient pagan god. Later this god became identified with the Devil. These scholars have attempted to trace the supposed practices of witches back to primitive religions. Such theories have been very popular. But serious students of witchcraft believe that real witch cults did not exist — or they were too few in number to be considered important.

Once the witchcraft hysteria got rolling, however, there were people who — without being accused — confessed to the crime of witchcraft. Even today when there is a sensational and well publicized crime, some innocent but mentally sick people confess to it. Police ignore these people. In the days of the witchcraft hysteria, they would have been killed.

Some of the people accused of witchcraft probably did practice witchcraft — in the old sense of the word, they were magicians. As we have said, making charms and medicinal potions was a common practice for centuries in Europe. It was considered dangerous to Christianity only when the Devil supposedly became involved.

The witches — that is, the magicians — were often old women who were outcasts from the community. They were

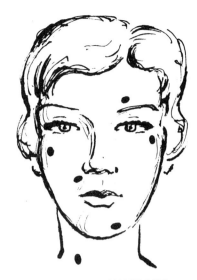

PROOF OF WITCHCRAFT
During the witchcraft madness, it was said that the Devil usually left a mark on the body of a witch. Face blemishes often were considered proof that a person had made a pact with the Devil.

A MATTER OF GEOGRAPHY
Opposite superstitions sometimes occur in different regions. For example, a man whose eyebrows meet over his nose is considered lucky among superstitious English and Chinese. But superstitious Germans and Icelanders would regard him as a witch.

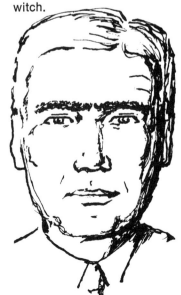

regarded with fear because of their strange ways and supposed power. Without friends or family, such people were easy targets when they were accused of the other kind of witchcraft, dealings with the Devil. Out of these times has come the modern picture of a witch as an old woman with a peaked hat who stirs strange ingredients in a bubbling cauldron.

Things that are not really present

Some magician-witches were skillful at mixing poisons and other dangerous drugs. At least a few of the deaths blamed on witchcraft could have been caused by poisons. Special plants were used to produce drugs that cause *hallucinations,* visions of things that are not really present.

The Spanish anthropologist Julio Caro Baroja believes that hallucinations produced by drugs accounted for some of the witchcraft stories. *Anthropology* is the science that studies the development of man, his customs, and his beliefs. Certain plant drugs, Dr. Baroja says, produce hallucinations that are depressing and frightening. These drugs can be prepared as ointments that are rubbed on the skin.

Most witches who confessed to flying did so because they were tortured. A few witches, however, actually believed that they flew with the help of a magic ointment. In the 17th century, a French doctor wrote a book describing plants and herbs that could cause such hallucinations. As years passed, other scientists and writers made the same point. Dr. Baroja concludes that it is drug ointments "and not flying brooms or animals which carry the witch into a world of fantasy and emotion."

Back to making charms

The fear of witchcraft that plunged Europe and colonial New England into hysteria is a well remembered part of our history. However, nobody but a superstitious few trembles today at the thought of witches. In fact, in the town of Salem, Massachusetts — scene of the last major outbreak of witch hunting in the world (mentioned earlier) — witches have become a source of local pride. The

MANY FORMS AND FACES
The Devil has been described in various ways. In this 1861 drawing, he appears as the horned god of witches.

A writer in A.D. 360 said that the Devil took the form of different animals and insects, such as "leopards, bears, horses, wolves, and scorpions."

One of the most dreaded forms of the Devil was his supposed appearance as an angel.

town symbol is an old crone in a peaked hat riding a broomstick.

Witchcraft, to a great extent today, means what it once did. A witch is again regarded as a magician and not as an anti-religious person who has made a pact with the Devil. Some communities in many countries, including America, still have local witches. As in the past, they are often old women who mix medicines and make charms for superstitious people.

Modern witches

In the late 18th century and in the 19th century, after the fear of witchcraft had disappeared, real Devil worshiping societies were formed. These societies took names like the Hellfire Club and were generally made up of university students. Many of the students who swore loyalty to the Devil were wealthy young men in search of "kicks" — new ways to enjoy themselves. Often their chief purpose was to shock people by defying accepted moral and religious beliefs.

A few societies that say they worship the Devil are still in existence. Their purpose is usually much the same — to outrage more conventional people — but not much attention is paid them. Although they claim their

AMERICAN WITCHCRAFT
The Salem, Massachusetts, witch trials began in 1692 in this house, which is still standing. It is now a museum. The bottle contains pins that the witches supposedly used to torment their victims.

In later years, some of the judges, jurors, and accusers connected with the trial publicly repented, confessing that they had been wrong.

By then, many of the accused witches either had been hanged or so persecuted that their lives were ruined.

BIBLICAL MEDIUM

People who believed in witches often quoted the Bible as evidence that witches existed — for example, the story of Saul's visit to the Witch of Endor.

Saul, King of the Jews, was deeply troubled about an attack by the Philistine army. He went to the Witch of Endor for help. At his request, she called up the spirit of Samuel, the previous ruler. Saul then asked Samuel for guidance.

In this story, as originally told in the Old Testament, the Witch of Endor was not actually a witch. She had not made a pact with the Devil but was acting as a medium (see page 19).

ceremonies are ancient, these claims do not stand up under investigation.

A number of witch societies and professional witches also exist today. In fact, interest in witchcraft is growing. Today's witches consider themselves to be "good" witches, not at all like their sinister sisters centuries ago. Since witchcraft is a fascinating subject, modern witches are occasionally written up in newspapers and magazines. Not many people, however, take such stories seriously. Witches also appear in leading roles in movies and television shows — a sure sign that the world is no longer afraid of them.

Chapter 6
DOWSING FOR WATER AND OTHER VALUABLES

Throughout the year, an old superstitious practice is repeated in farmers' fields in every state in the United States. A man with a forked stick gripped tightly in his hands walks back and forth slowly over the field. He is looking for underground water and the best place to dig a well. The stick in his hands begins to quiver or suddenly points downward — this is supposed to be the sign that water is not too far beneath the surface.

American farmers are the most advanced in the world. Many of them have studied scientific farming methods in college. Yet when farmers have to find water, a large percentage of them will turn to the unscientific practice of *water dowsing,* or *water witching* — using a forked stick or other object to find water. In the South and West, the practice is usually called *witching;* in the Northeast, it is called *dowsing.* Other less common names are *water divining, water wishing, water smelling,* and *witch wriggling.*

Why use a dowser?

The idea that some people have the ability to find underground water with a forked stick is one of the most widely held superstitions in America today. In many parts of the country, hiring a dowser to find water is as common as hiring a plumber to stop a leak or an electrician to repair a light switch.

Drilling a well is expensive; the deeper the well, the more expensive it is. A farmer can spend anywhere from $3,000 to $15,000 on an irrigation well. It is much cheaper if he starts drilling where water is near the surface. But often there is no accurate way of telling where the best water supply is.

Most rural communities have someone who claims to be able to find water with a forked stick. Usually this water dowser will work for nothing or for a small fee.

SEARCHING FOR WATER
There are about 25,000 water dowsers in the United States today. Most of them live in rural areas, where farmers and home owners often have to supply their own water.

WATER DRILL

Drilling for water may take a day or a few weeks. The time spent depends on the rockiness of the soil and how deep the water is below the surface of the earth. Well depths vary from less than 50 feet to many thousand feet.

Most home wells yield a few gallons of water a minute. However, large industrial and public wells pump water thousands of gallons a minute.

Since the farmer has no idea where to start drilling, he is ready to let the dowser pick the spot for him. If water is found near the surface, the farmer will probably be convinced that dowsing works. If the dowser picks a poor spot — without water or where the water is far below the surface — the farmer will be disappointed. But he will have no way of knowing whether he would have made a better or worse choice without the aid of the dowser.

Water dowsing is most common in areas where water is hardest to find. In the face of uncertainty, people often turn to traditional superstitious practices. This is especially true where problems, like finding water, exist for which scientific help is often not available.

What can science do?

Although many people use a dowser, not all of them are convinced that dowsing works. Most farmers undoubtedly know of cases where dowsing has not worked very well, and they know it has never been proven scientifically. But even the best geological help is of limited use in finding underground water. *Geology* is the science that studies the history and structure of the earth's crust.

There are a number of delicate scientific instruments that can explore underground features. Such instruments can, for example, help to locate underground rock structures where the probability of finding oil is rather high. But as yet no foolproof way exists for finding underground water without digging for it.

Geologists are unable to tell a farmer exactly where the best spot is to sink a well. Many farmers feel that they have nothing to lose if they call in a dowser. One county farm official from Iowa commented, "Not too many have faith in witching [dowsing], but people here use it in the absence of any other method of locating water."

How dowsing began

The history of water dowsing is unclear. Some believers say dowsing goes back to the biblical story in which Moses strikes a rock with his rod and water pours forth. But

IS PETROLEUM BELOW?
To find out, an explosive is placed in a hole in the earth. When the explosive goes off, it creates a shock wave that is recorded on a seismograph, an instrument that detects and measures earthquakes.

The seismograph record shows the different layers of material below the earth's surface. It may also reveal an underground deposit of petroleum. As yet, such scientific methods have not been effective in finding water.

its history can only be traced accurately to 16th century Germany. One opponent of dowsing at that time was the Swiss-German physician Paracelsus (1493-1541). If the dowser's stick is right once, he said, it deceives 10 or 20 times. From Germany, dowsing spread throughout Europe and the United States. Different forms of dowsing are used in parts of Asia and Africa. Whether they all came from the same tradition or were developed independently, we do not know.

Originally, forked sticks were used to locate metal ores. Some dowsers would begin their search saying, "In the name of the Father, Son, and Holy Ghost, how many fathoms is it from here to the ore?" Religious authorities, however, did not approve of dowsing. They thought it was evil magic. More than one dowser found himself in prison charged with the dangerous crime of witchcraft or *sorcery* (the use of supernatural powers through the help of evil spirits). By the 18th century, the religious persecution of dowsers had disappeared. Dowsing became an accepted practice, at least among those who thought that a forked stick in the hands of the right man would point to water.

81

**DOWSING MORE
THAN 400 YEARS AGO**

The dowser in this 16th century picture is searching for metals. Did everybody in this period believe in dowsing? Apparently not. George Agricola, the writer of the book in which this picture appears, pointed out:

"Among miners there are many great arguments about the forked twig, for some say it is of the greatest use to them in discovering veins, while others deny this."

Not the stick but the dowser

Even today, a dowser usually prefers to work with a forked stick made from a branch. If no branches are available, other materials can be used — coat hangers, baling wire, steel files, pliers, or any one of a number of specially made dowsing gadgets. The tool, often called a *dowsing rod,* does not seem to matter — it is the dowser that is important. According to those who believe in dowsing, not just anyone can locate water. Certain people are supposed to be born with a gift for dowsing. The gift is said to be passed on from father to son.

It is common for skeptics (people who doubt or disbelieve) to dismiss those who practice dowsing as uneducated — but this is not true. A typical dowser is as

well educated as the average man in his community. In addition, there are highly educated men who believe in and even practice dowsing.

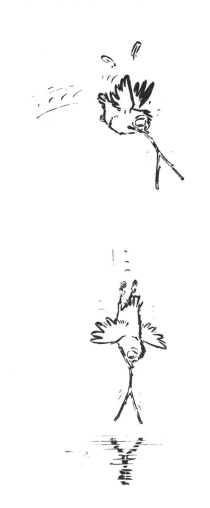

Most are honest

Most dowsers do not attempt to explain why dowsing supposedly works. As practical minded men, they say all they care about is finding water. Some will offer a religious explanation — for example, the power of dowsing has been passed on from Moses in some mysterious way. Others develop elaborate theories that sound scientific but actually are not. One such theory is that underground substances, including water, are surrounded by electromagnetic fields. These fields somehow are supposed to affect the muscles of the dowser.

Many skeptics denounce dowsing as an out-and-out fake. They say that the dowser intentionally makes the rod jump when he finds a likely looking spot. Probably some dowsers are fakes. But most of them move their rods without planning to do so beforehand.

If the dowser is honest, how can we explain the movement of his rod? One likely answer points to unconscious feelings. *Conscious* thoughts are deliberate and intended, and we are aware of them. The opposite is true of *unconscious* feelings. They are not deliberate and not intended, and we are mostly unaware that we have them.

If the clues are right

Some scientists think that the movement of the dowsing rod is controlled by an unconscious feeling of the dowser — thus the dowser moves his rod without knowing why. However, what makes the dowser point his rod at a particular spot on the ground? Here is one answer suggested by these scientists:

Underground water may betray its presence by clues on the earth's surface, such as certain rocks, the color of the soil, and the shape of the ground. The dowser is usually a local man, well acquainted with the earth's

83

HARGREAVES

surface in the area. After years of experience, he may have become an expert at recognizing the clues that indicate water — even though he is not consciously aware of them.

When the dowser is seeking water, he walks around until the clues indicate a good place to drill. While walking, he grips the rod very tightly. All it takes is a slight change in the tension of his muscles to cause the rod to shake or point down. If the clues are right, the unconscious feeling "water is here" is signaled to the muscles of his hands. Without being aware of the signal, he moves these muscles, and the rod points downward.

Other unconscious movements

Unconscious muscular movements have played a large part in the history of superstition. The messages produced by the Ouija board (see photograph) or by automatic writing are often the result of unconscious muscular movements. *Automatic writing* is the production of a written message by a person who does not consciously know what he is writing. Some mediums (see page 19) claim to receive messages from the spirit world this way. While the medium is in trance, she holds a pencil over paper. The pencil is supposedly guided by the spirit that the medium is in contact with. Often the writing that appears is quite different from the normal writing of the medium.

84

Magicians, too, work with unconscious muscular movements, using a method called *muscle reading*. One trick that depends on muscle reading is finding a pin that has been concealed in a room. The magician is outside the room when the pin is hidden. Then he enters and "leads" one of the spectators to the pin. Actually, the spectator is leading the magician.

The magician places his hand on the spectator's arm. As the spectator gets closer to the hidden pin or farther away from it, his muscles tense or relax. The magician is guided by these muscle movements as clearly as a plane following a directional beam. All this time the spectator has no idea of the signals his muscles are sending out.

"Something moved it"

Even if we do not know how a magician performs his magic, most of us recognize that he uses tricks and skills rather than supernatural powers. When a dowser's rod jumps, however, a feeling is often created that something supernatural has taken place.

Consider a skeptic watching a dowser at work. "I just don't believe that stick jumped by itself," he says. "You must have helped it." The dowser shakes his head seriously and hands the skeptic the forked stick. "See for yourself," he says. "Hold the stick tightly, and walk to the place where I located water."

DOWSING ROD VS. THE LAWS OF CHANCE
A metal object was hidden under 1 of the 6 cups. Then this special dowsing rod was used to try to find the object.

Several hundred tests were made. Each time the object was placed under a different cup.

The object was located 1 out of every 6 tries — a result that agrees with the laws of chance. In other words, the rod performed no better or worse than guessing.

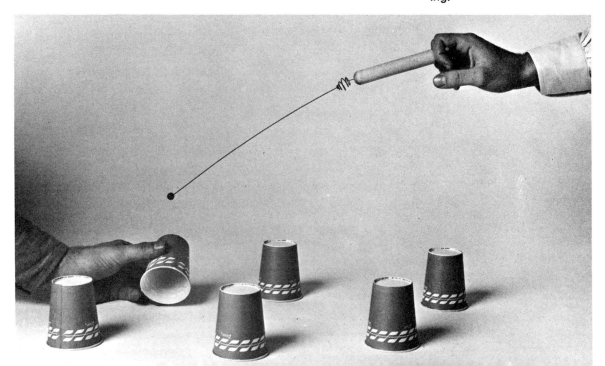

CHANGES THAT OCCUR WITHOUT OUR KNOWLEDGE

The idea of unconscious muscular movements at first may seem strange. It becomes more understandable when we realize that many of the body's activities are changed by thoughts and emotions.

Mostly, we are not aware that these changes are taking place. Some of them, however, can be measured by instruments like the polygraph (lie detector).

Each pen in the polygraph at the right is recording a change in a different body activity. The wavy ink lines show how large or small the change is.

From the top down, the body activities being measured are these: respiration, electrical skin resistance, blood pressure, oxygenation of the blood.

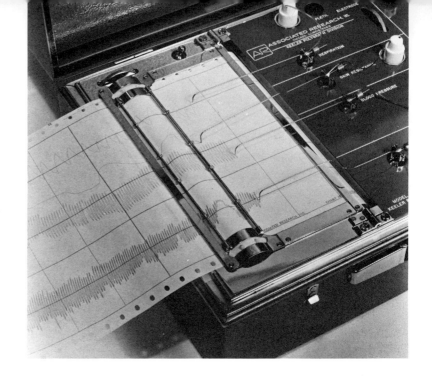

The skeptic imitates the dowser's grip and even his walk. As he approaches the place where water is supposed to be, he slowly becomes more excited. He grips the stick tighter and tighter. The idea that he may actually be standing over water grows in his mind. He may be shocked to feel the stick suddenly jump in his hands, although he thought he was holding it firmly. "Something moved it," he yells. The skeptic used the same unconscious muscular movements as the dowser. These movements were probably triggered by his increasing excitement and nervousness — and by the dowser's honest "see-for-yourself" invitation, which probably planted a seed of belief that water had actually been located.

Two reasons for success

Unconscious muscular movements have been understood for centuries. But water dowsing is as popular as ever because dowsers sometimes do find water. Their success, when it does occur, is generally based on either of these 2 reasons:

1. Dowsers may unconsciously recognize features on the earth's surface that indicate underground water.
2. If a well is dug deep enough almost anywhere, there is a good chance of bringing up underground water.

All dowsers say they can pick the best spot to drill a well. Some also say they can predict the depth at which water will be found and the amount of water available. These claims are not supported by solid evidence. In fact, in the few scientific tests of dowsers that have been carried out, even their ability to find the best spot for a well was not proven.

The mysterious doodlebug

Not all dowsers seek water. Dowsing devices have been used in an attempt to locate many underground items, such as buried treasure, pipelines, wires, and oil. A dowser looking for oil may work with a *doodlebug* instead of a dowsing rod. Many such fake devices exist. One of the simplest is a pendulum consisting of a ball hanging on a string. When this doodlebug is above an underground reservoir of oil, the ball is supposed to swing in a particular way.

More complicated doodlebugs are usually said to operate on mysterious principles known only to their inventors. Doodlebugs have often been used to cheat people who are anxious to find oil on their land. Although the water dowser charges a low fee or no fee at all, the oil dowser may take as much as $1,000 for the services of his mysterious doodlebug.

The sex indicator

A ball-and-string pendulum is often sold in novelty shops as a *sex indicator*. The pendulum is held over a

MICHAEL FARADAY INVESTIGATES
A group of people are seated around a table. Their fingers touch the top of the table. Slowly the table begins to turn. The people are convinced that a spirit is turning the table.

The time? It could be the present, but it is the 1850's in England. The brilliant scientist Michael Faraday is present. His investigation reveals that unconscious muscular movements cause the table to turn.

He concluded that the table turned because of "mechanical pressure exerted inadvertently [unintentionally] by the turner."

MILITARY DOWSING
These United States Marines in Vietnam are looking for buried explosives with mine sweepers. Several times, when mine sweepers were not available, the marines used dowsing rods.

A physicist, who works for the marines and is one of the few scientists who believe in dowsing, admitted that the forked twig was not very successful in Vietnam.

87

DOES THE
PENDULUM WORK?

You can easily make the pendulum needed for the experiment discussed on this and the next page.

Almost anything will serve as a weight, for example, a large marble, a metal nut, a fishing sinker, or a pebble. A piece of string or an inexpensive necklace will allow the weight to swing freely.

You may be able to tie the string or necklace to the weight. If you have to glue them, epoxy cement is satisfactory because it forms a strong bond.

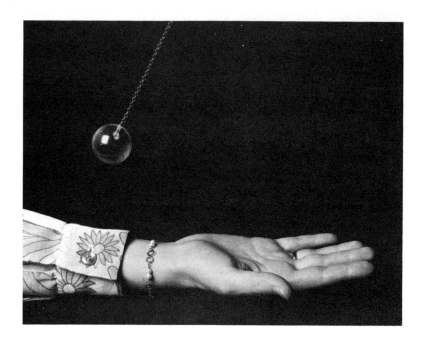

person's hand. The motion of the ball is then supposed to indicate the sex of the person. If the person is male, the ball will swing back and forth; if female, the ball will swing in a circle. Apparently the sex indicator works — or does it?

The person holding the sex indicator is really doing the work, though he may not be aware of it. For example, if you were holding the pendulum above a boy's hand, you would probably swing the ball back and forth. Most likely you would not realize that you were controlling the movement of the ball. You would be exerting an unconscious muscular movement similar to that exerted by the water dowser on his forked stick.

Every time or 1 time out of 2?

How could you convince yourself that it is really your unconscious feelings and not the pendulum that guides the movement of the ball? One good way is to introduce a controlled experiment. In science, a *controlled experiment* checks the results of another experiment by leaving out a condition that is being tested.

T h i s question-and-answer game is similar to the Ouija board (described on page 84). Perhaps the word *game* is not suitable, for the people are serious.

The letters of the alphabet are positioned around the edge of the table. Everybody places a finger on the water glass in the center.

A question is asked. The glass, with all the fingers on it, moves to various letters of the alphabet. It stops here and there to make up words that provide an answer.

Usually, in groups like this, 1 person will push the glass by unconscious muscular movements. It may even be the person who asked the question.

The condition you leave out in this controlled experiment is your knowledge of the sex of the person whose hand is held out. If you do not know whether that person is a boy or girl, you will not be able to unconsciously guide the movement of the ball. A blindfold is all you require.

If you use the pendulum without a blindfold, the ball will probably swing correctly every time — back and forth for a male, in a circle for a female.

If you use the pendulum with a blindfold, guessing rather than unconscious thought will guide the movement of the ball. You have 2 choices — male or female — and 1 guess each time. Chances are you will guess right 1 time out of 2, or half the time.

The action of unconscious muscular movements is shown clearly in the experiment with the sex indicator. These same movements are used in water dowsing. Yet many people still believe that water dowsers possess some special power. And, as we have seen, people today continue to hold other superstitions. How can we guard against being superstitious? We will explore this question in the next chapter.

Chapter 7
MAN'S POWER TO THINK

In our story so far, we have uncovered many reasons that explain why people have superstitious beliefs. Some of these reasons are tradition, fear, ignorance, habit, ritual, a need to find answers to troubling situations, anxiety, and a desire to influence events that are beyond control.

Can you explain the superstitions we have investigated by matching them against one or more reasons on the list? You may discover that *a need to find answers to troubling situations* appears more than the others. Are there any other reasons you think should be added to the list?

Disaster superstitions

Once we have examined these reasons, we can better understand why people react so strongly to *disaster superstitions*. When a powerful force in nature — like an earthquake — is related to a superstition, the result can be tragic. Disaster superstitions frighten people for a long time and sometimes cause them to change their lives against their own interests.

A black cat walking across one's path, the supposed appearance of a ghost in a dark graveyard, and the spilling of salt are brief events. But disaster superstitions last for years and sometimes throughout a person's life. Let us look into one of these superstitions closely.

During 1968 and the early months of 1969, wild rumors spread that the state of California was going to be destroyed in a great earthquake before April, 1969. Books, articles, and even songs were written about the coming earthquake. Few people openly admitted that they took these rumors seriously. But some left the state late in March "just to be on the safe side."

April came and went, and California was not destroyed. The entire earthquake scare was a disaster superstition, nothing more. How had these rumors started? Why did so many people believe them? And why did some people refuse to admit that their beliefs had been wrong?

SUPERSTITION OR SERIOUS STUDY?

The Roman blacksmith-god Vulcan was thought to have his workshop inside fiery mountains. *Volcano* is derived from his name. Although belief in Vulcan has disappeared, superstitions about volcanoes persist.

Superstitions offer us little help if we are faced with the possibility of a natural disaster. Better approaches are available.

For example, the government of Costa Rica called in United Nations experts to study Irazu Volcano, shown here. From such studies, we may learn how to predict — and possibly control — the eruptions of volcanoes.

The San Andreas Fault

Earthquakes are fairly common in California. In 1906, large portions of the city of San Francisco were destroyed by one of the worst earthquakes in modern times. Many smaller earthquakes have shaken the state since.

Most of these earthquakes have taken place along a 600-mile crack in the earth's surface called the San Andreas Fault. Scientists do not know exactly how earthquakes are caused, nor can they accurately predict when earthquakes will occur. They have, however, observed that the tension (pull) between the two sides of the fault is increasing. This tension may well cause another major earthquake in California. But when the earthquake will take place, scientists cannot say — it might be next week or a few hundred years from now. Nor can they predict how large or small the earthquake will be.

Although the scientists did not make any definite predictions, their statements about the possibility of an

DISASTER THAT LEADS TO SUPERSTITION
During the past century, earthquakes in the United States have killed close to 1,600 people and destroyed about $2.3 billion in property.

Other countries, like Japan, have suffered far more severely. The photograph shows buildings damaged by the great San Francisco earthquake of 1906.

earthquake were reported on television and in newspapers and magazines. What they really pointed out was that the situation was no more alarming than it had ever been. Some people were calmed by what the scientists said. However, any discussion about earthquakes is likely to make a number of people nervous. For this reason, there were some who became increasingly worried.

The sleeping prophet

Definite predictions of earthquakes did come from other sources. In the early 1940's, a man named Edgar Cayce predicted that the world would be shaken by a series of major catastrophes. Among these would be a huge earthquake in California.

Edgar Cayce has become known as *the sleeping prophet* because he made many of his predictions when he was in a trancelike state. He died in 1944, but today his predictions are more popular than ever, and he has many followers. Edgar Cayce's predictions are sometimes vague. A number of people interpreted his words to mean that the catastrophes would begin in 1968 or 1969. (Mr. Cayce

WITHOUT WARNING

The severe California earthquake of February, 1971, had not been predicted by either scientists or prophets. More than 60 people were killed, and property damage reached about $1 billion.

The quake was not triggered by the San Andreas Fault but by a smaller fault nearby. The elevated highway that collapsed, shown in the photograph, is north of the San Fernando Valley.

TREATED THE SICK
People often came to Edgar Cayce with health problems. While in a trancelike state, he would diagnose their illnesses and prescribe remedies.

Were his medical statements correct? Today, more than 25 years after Mr. Cayce's death, there is still disagreement on the answer to this question.

"MAYBE WE'LL MISS THE CHEMISTRY EXAM...."

also predicted that New York would suffer an earthquake. That prediction never caught the public's imagination because New Yorkers do not worry about earthquakes — New York is not an earthquake area.)

Follow the leader

There are always a small number of people in all parts of the world who claim they can *prophesy* — that is, foresee the future. Some of these prophets are frauds. Others honestly believe they have the power to make predictions. For example, Edgar Cayce's predictions have been strongly criticized. Yet even his critics regard Mr. Cayce as a man who truly believed — as do his followers today — that he had the ability to look into the future.

When a well known prophet like Edgar Cayce makes a prediction, lesser prophets follow him. This happened with Mr. Cayce's catastrophe predictions for California. Many predictions began to circulate that a destructive earthquake would take place in California in 1968 or 1969.

California is earthquake country. It is not surprising that some earthquakes occurred in 1968 — as they do every year. The United States Coast and Geodetic Survey reported that in 1968 (as in most years) there was "an absence of severe damage and casualties." The prophets were not discouraged. They were more vigorous than ever in predicting that the catastrophe would take place in 1969. It never did.

News stories and jokes

Newspapers and magazines often print stories about the predictions of a prophet. Television can bring the prophet right into homes. When many prophets begin predicting the same event, even more stories appear about them. There were so many predictions of a great California earthquake that it became a major news story.

Some stories about the predicted earthquake seriously criticized the prophecies or made fun of them. As the stories spread, comedians on television joked about the earthquake. Discussion programs on radio treated the subject with a sense of fun. But the stories and jokes —

even though they were humorous — kept the prophecies alive.

A family might laugh at a television comedian's funny treatment of the earthquake. But when the program was over, it would not be unusual for somebody to quote the old saying, "Where there's smoke, there's fire."

People began talking about the earthquake more and more. And the more they talked, the more serious the prophecies seemed to be. Where then do all the jokes about the earthquake lead us? We still do not have enough facts to provide a definite answer. However, we certainly can think about this possibility: Joking about a superstition can make it grow stronger — creating more believers than doubters.

Turn around

Psychologists have often tested the ability of people to remember what they have read or heard. These tests have shown that most of us remember things we agree with more than we remember things we disagree with.

EARTHQUAKE EXPECTANCY

Scientists still cannot forecast when an earthquake will take place. However, the U.S. Coast and Geodetic Survey has rated the continental United States for possible earthquake damage.

On the map, white areas have no reasonable expectancy of earthquakes. Major earthquakes may occur in the black areas. Minor and moderate earthquakes may occur in the 2 gray areas.

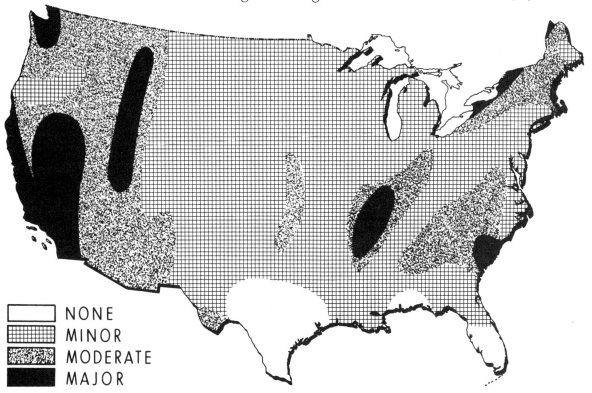

☐ NONE
▦ MINOR
▨ MODERATE
■ MAJOR

A person might read a long article that was generally critical of the earthquake predictions — but that also stated there might be an earthquake. Let us assume he was inclined to believe in the power of prophecy or that he really worried about earthquakes. He would probably tend to remember only those parts of the article that supported the earthquake predictions. Thus, in his mind, he would be turning around a critical article so that it supported his beliefs.

Why should rumors continue?

Rumors about the coming earthquake had become so unreal that some earthquake experts felt that they had to tell the public their side. As a rule, experts make rather quiet public statements, but one group did not pull its punches. They said: "Wild predictions of disastrous earthquakes — issued by self-proclaimed oracles [prophets] and other visionaries — are not supported by scientific evidence and are frightening many Californians needlessly." However, even such strong statements did not stop the rumors. Many people did not seem to believe the experts. Why?

Remember that one reason the farmer believes the water dowser is that the dowser can be definite and say, "Dig here." Similarly, the prophet, predicting an earthquake, can say, "There will be an earthquake on April 4." A scientist who studies earthquakes, however, does not have enough facts to be that definite. He can only say that there is no particular reason to believe that an earthquake will occur on that day. He also may point out that there probably will be an earthquake at some time, but he does not know exactly when.

An ancient attitude

There are numerous natural disasters every year. Some are very severe, but they are still limited in power. For example, scientists do not agree with the modern prophets who say that an earthquake could be powerful enough to sink the entire state of California into the ocean. But

**ATLANTIS —
A DISASTER LEGEND**
The earliest record we have of the legend of Atlantis was written by the Greek philosopher Plato, who lived from about 427 B.C. to 347 B.C. Since Plato, thousands of articles and books on Atlantis have appeared. The story they generally tell is this:

A beautiful island or continent named Atlantis once existed in the Atlantic Ocean. Its people were superior to any alive today. Then a great earthquake caused Atlantis, with its people and cities, to sink beneath the water.

Many who believe in the legend say that another great earthquake will cause Atlantis to rise again. Plato thought that Atlantis was located near the mouth of the Mediterranean Sea. Several other locations have been suggested, among them the waters off an island in the Bahamas, shown in the photograph.

PUNISHMENT

The idea that natural disasters are a form of punishment has a long history. It is illustrated, for example, in the biblical account of an earthquake destroying the wicked cities of Sodom and Gomorrah.

many people believed just that — and they thought it was going to happen.

Another attitude that caused some people to believe that California would be destroyed was that the state deserved to be punished. The Bible tells how wicked people and even wicked cities were suddenly destroyed by God. The idea that the wicked pay for their crimes is still very powerful. Anyone with this belief who thought California was a wicked state would be inclined to believe that it would be destroyed.

The man who left

How did people feel after the predicted earthquake failed to occur. If a man did not believe the prediction, he might be happy that he had been correct and that nothing terrible had happened. Another man who had been worried but who continued to live his life normally

CHECKING
FOR EARTHQUAKES

As many as 500,000 earthquakes may occur in a year — most of them extremely small.

They only can be detected and measured with sensitive instruments like the seismograph (see photograph).

During any year, 1 or 2 major earthquakes can be expected in populated areas throughout the world.

might feel greatly relieved. But what about the man who, believing in the prediction, quit his job and left the state?

Probably he, too, will feel relief that California has not been destroyed. But another, more disturbing state of mind can develop — a feeling that he was foolish to change his way of life because of a false prediction. This feeling is hard to live with. He will want to eliminate the distress that people generally have when they feel foolish about their actions.

Most of us can reduce or get rid of a foolish feeling by admitting to ourselves that we were wrong. Usually we also promise ourselves that we will not act the same way again. However, a deeply superstitious person often cannot face the fact that one of his strong beliefs has been proven false. Instead, he will *rationalize,* that is, make up logical sounding but incorrect reasons to explain why the prediction did not come true.

"Just wait and see"

Do you remember the fox in Aesop's fable? The story of the fox's rationalization has been told for some 2,500 years. The fox kept jumping for a bunch of grapes that hung high above him on a branch. After he realized that he could not reach the grapes, he said that he really did not want them because they were probably sour.

SOUR GRAPES
Not strong enough to reach so high
He salved his grief while going by:
Just as I thought before I'd seen;
Those grapes aren't ripe at all, but green.

The deeply superstitious man will act in much the same way. He will convince himself that since the original prediction was vague, the exact date of the earthquake had been figured incorrectly. In his mind, the prediction will remain completely believable. The earthquake, as he now sees it, will definitely occur at some time in the future. "Just wait and see," he may say. "The California earthquake is bound to come next year." Of course, that is what he was saying last year.

The psychologist Leon Festinger studied people who believed deeply in something that proved to be wrong.

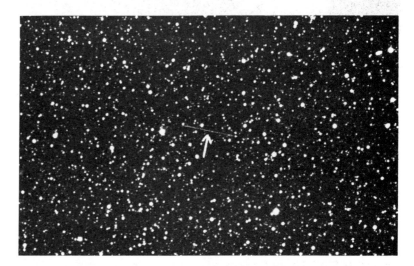

FLIGHT WITHOUT CAUSE
In June, 1968, the asteroid Icarus passed within 4 million miles of the earth. Its path is the streak of light to which the arrow points in the photograph.

Astronomers emphasized that there was no danger that Icarus would collide with the earth. However, a number of people did not believe the astronomers.

Fearing that a collision would take place, many of these people fled for safety to high altitudes in the mountain area of Boulder, Colorado.

He concluded that such people often feel "If more and more people can be persuaded that the system of belief is correct, then clearly it must, after all, be correct." Thus many people who have been completely wrong in a belief continue to talk and act as if they had been right all along. In fact, they sometimes try harder than ever to convince those with a different view.

How can we judge?

Occasionally we are faced with a large and even frightening idea — like the predictions of the California earthquake. Or we have to think about ideas that may seem strange to us — like the advice of an astrologer or spirit medium. How can we judge if these ideas deserve serious consideration or are pure superstition? Unfortunately, such judgments are not always easy to make. We can often think more clearly, however, if we test strange ideas with rules of reason, like these:

1. Find out where and why the idea started.
2. Before you accept or reject the idea, consider all arguments for and against it.
3. Be skeptical about information from people who claim to have "secret" or "supernatural" sources.
4. Do not believe the idea just because it is popular and all of your friends may be talking about it.
5. Do not believe everything you read. An idea that has been supported in a newspaper or magazine article is not necessarily true. Newspapers and magazines sometimes unknowingly print stories that are inaccurate or even silly.

SANTA CLAUS OR THE GREAT PUMPKIN
Some people who have their own superstitions strongly reject the superstitions of others. Cartoonist Schulz gently kids such people when he says that it doesn't matter whether you believe in Santa Claus or The Great Pumpkin — "just so you're sincere!"

PEANUTS ®   By Charles M. Schulz

Man's power to think

If rules like these had been followed throughout human history, our ancestors would not have led such superstitious lives. Nor would the superstitions that exist today still confuse and mislead us. Certainly the many cruelties committed by superstitious people would have been avoided. As an example, we only have to consider the 200,000 people who were tortured and killed in the witchcraft madness in Europe.

When we read or think about it, the destruction of 200,000 innocent lives still troubles us. But there is a deeper horror behind these deaths: the effect that superstition can have on the human mind. In *The Encyclopedia of Witchcraft and Demonology*, Professor Rossell Hope Robbins discusses this effect in a statement worth remembering: "Nothing about witchcraft is more ominous than the suppression and destruction of man's power to think and his right to ask questions."

REASON
Today a witch is a figure of fun at Halloween. Just a few hundred years ago, however, she represented a dreaded force of evil. This change suggests 2 conclusions:

The first is that we have made progress in rejecting superstition, perhaps more in the past few hundred years than in the past few thousand.

The second is that we can continue to make progress, as we have done in the past, by using reason as a guide to understanding the mysterious.

useful information

imaginary creatures

that live in the world of the supernatural

A special section

Written by Gene Liberty and illustrated by Jacolyn A. Mott

The next 8 pages explore a world that does not exist. At one time, this world — inhabited by supernatural creatures — was real for practically everybody. For some, it is still real today. Most of us, however, do not believe in ghosts, elves, werewolves, and the like.

Our ancestors invented supernatural creatures to explain mysteries in nature — thunder, growth, an unusual death, the moods of the sea. We share with our ancestors the common bond of being human. Thus we can understand the fear and hope and imagination that went into their struggle to interpret the unknown.

Because of this understanding, we are enriched by learning about the supernatural world even when we believe that it does not exist. It reveals what we have been in the past and teaches us something about ourselves as we are now.

BANSHEE

The mournful song and weeping of a banshee are not welcome sounds in Ireland. A banshee is a fairy who usually looks like a beautiful woman but sometimes takes the form of a witchlike hag. In Irish legends, the appearance of a banshee means that somebody will soon die.

BROWNIE

When you give a brownie a gift, it will make him go away. And who would want to do that? Brownies are the most helpful of the little people, as the old English and Scottish superstitions tell us. Should a brownie go to live in a house, he will do the chores at night and provide protection against unfriendly spirits.

If the brownie is criticized or otherwise annoyed, trouble is on the way. He will break dishes, spoil crops, tangle hair, and give sleepers nightmares. Perhaps now is the time to give the brownie a gift, for the moment to part company has come. Brownies hate to receive gifts, and the little fellow with the brown wrinkled face will wrap himself in his brown hood and cloak and leave.

DEMON

And neither the angels in Heaven above
Nor the demons down under the sea
Can ever dissever my soul from the soul
Of the beautiful Annabel Lee.

Throughout the world, good and evil are often represented by supernatural beings. In these lovely, haunting lines by Edgar Allan Poe, angels are the forces of good, and demons are the forces of evil. Between both, one might think, is the widest possible difference. But this is not wholly true.

Some legends say that demons were fallen angels, that is, angels who were banished from heaven because they had committed unworthy acts. It is understandable, then, that among the Jews of biblical times, all demons were not evil. Some had angel-like qualities and were helpful to mankind.

In India, demons were also linked to goodness but in a strangely different way. The gods of the old legends represented the forces of good. They fought terrible battles — which they sometimes lost — against evil demons. Yet demons often received their powers of magic from the gods themselves. Thus, at times, the gods provided the very powers that were used to defeat them.

Today in Christian countries, demons are rarely connected in any way with the idea of goodness. Two general meanings have developed:

1. A demon is a supernatural being who brings trouble and misfortune to mankind. In this sense, a malicious dwarf can be called a demon.

2. A demon is a devil, one of the beings ruled by Satan. As used here, *devil* and *demon* have the same meaning. The word *Devil* spelled with a capital *D* usually refers to Satan, the ruler of Hell. His subjects — who serve as messengers and assistants — are demons, or *devils,* spelled with a small *d.*

DWARF

Dwarves are the most industrious of the little people. They live inside a fairy-tale world of mountains and hills, where they work with marvelous skill as metalsmiths and jewelers.

Most dress in gray or green and wear pointed red caps. They have human faces, leathery skin, and long beards. Their stride often is wobbly because they tend to have flat feet or have their feet on backwards.

Like other little people, dwarves enjoy feasting and dancing, especially when the moon is full. If a dwarf is in a good mood — perhaps after a delicious meal — he may give a human a gift that will turn into gold.

Usually, dwarves are kind to people. But there are exceptions. Many German dwarves, for example, bring grief to the people they meet. And all dwarves have some bad habits, like stealing or playing tricks.

A human with a problem, the legends tell us, often is helped when he turns to a dwarf for advice. Dwarves have 2 qualities important in a good adviser — wisdom and the ability to see into the future.

105

ELF

Can you hear the music of the elves in these lines by the poet Alfred Tennyson?

O sweet and far from cliff and scar
The horns of Elfland faintly blowing!

The elves lived in the woods, where they spent much of their time dancing. These tiny beings in human form sometimes used their magic to be helpful and kind to humans. But they were filled with mischief and could trick a human into trouble as easily as lead him to good fortune.

Not all elves were kindly or mischievous. Some were feared because they had terrifying powers that could cause injury and all sorts of other misfortunes.

Diseases of cattle were often blamed on elves. In England, such diseases were thought to have come from wounds made by stone arrowheads found on the ground. The arrowheads were regarded as evidence that the elves existed. Actually they were made by the people of the New Stone Age, who lived some 6,000 to 11,000 years ago.

FAIRY

What does a fairy look like? Two of the best-known storybook fairies are Tinker Bell in *Peter Pan* and the fairy godmother in *Cinderella*. Tinker Bell is a small ball of light, and the fairy godmother resembles an adult woman.

Many fairies dress in green and may even have green skin and green hair. Some people consider brownies and dwarves (discussed separately in this section) to be fairies. One famous Welsh fairy looks like a black bat.

Fairies vary greatly in appearance and are part of the legends of many countries. They are usually invisible unless they choose to reveal themselves. Their power permits them to see into the future and to perform good or harmful acts. Often they are mischievous, and a gift of gold may turn into dried leaves.

Some fairies live in hills, under piles of stones, and even in human homes. Others live in the kingdom of the fairies, which they occasionally leave. In their travels — like all fairies — they tend to become involved in the problems of people.

GENIE

Two thousand years before the biblical creation of Adam, genies were formed from fire. These supernatural creatures of Arabic legend were of 2 types — good and evil. Their home was a mountain range of emerald that circled the world.

When genies came among humans, they often took the form of animals or insects. Or they chose to be invisible. Sometimes genies served humans and aided them with magic, as did the 2 genies in the story of Aladdin. The words *djinni* (plural:*djinn*) and *jinni* (plural:*jinn*) have the same meaning as *genie.*

GHOST

Which supernatural beings walk, eat, drive cars, ride horses, play musical instruments, read, smile, and talk? They have the characteristics of a human — and more.

When they walk, they leave no footprints. When they talk, the sound cannot be recorded.

When they leave, they may disappear suddenly or just fade away.

And when they want to voice a feeling, they can groan, moan, howl, yell, whisper, sigh, or scream.

At one time or another, practically every people in the world has believed in them. Many still do today. In addition to their most widely-used name, they are often called phantoms, specters, shades, spooks, phantasms, apparitions, revenants, haunts, spirits, or presences.

They are said to be the souls, or spirits, of dead people (or sometimes dead animals) that could not rest. Often they return to the world of the living because they have to complete some unfinished mission. For example, they may have to provide information that only they know, punish a wrongdoer, or warn somebody of danger.

If they committed suicide or lost their lives violently, say through murder or an accident, they may come back to the place they died. There they will possibly re-enact the scenes of their deaths again and again. Or they may wander about as if trying to live out the years that were unexpectedly lost.

They are the best known of all supernatural beings. In fact, they supposedly live in so many castles, churches, and homes in England that they have become a tourist attraction. Headless Hunter, Laughing Lady, Angry Bishop, Sad Singer, and Gardener's Son are just a few of the names given to them by the English in different locales.

At one English castle, a message was scratched on the main gate. Some claimed that the gatekeeper had written the message to encourage interest in the castle. Others felt that the first letter in each word of the message identified the writer: Go home or suffer terribly.

GHOUL

In Arabic legend, a ghoul is an evil spirit or demon that robs graves and feeds on corpses. This meaning has broadened to include people. The word *ghoul* now also describes a person who is a grave robber or who delights in evil acts.

GIANT

In some legends, the first form of life to appear on earth — even before the gods — was the giants. Their immense bodies and usually violent natures reflected the wild, harsh earth when it began to form. They often were the masters of powerful forces, such as hurricanes, thunder, volcanoes, and earthquakes.

Many giants were cannibals, like Grendel, who appears in the 9th-century heroic story *Beowulf.* The giant gods of the Iroquois Indians were feared because they, too, would eat men. In the old English tale *Jack and the Beanstalk,* the young adventurer Jack knew that he had to escape a similar fate when he heard the giant cry out:

> *Fee-fi-fo-fum*
> *I smell the blood of an Englishman*
> *Be he live or be he dead*
> *I'll grind his bones to make my bread*

Here and there a kindly and wise giant existed. One of these was Mimir, who lived in the water. Even the great Odin, chief of the Scandinavian and German gods, turned to Mimir for knowledge and advice.

Nor did all giants resemble humans. Many of them had the forms of animals, birds, or monsters. For example, some Scandinavian giants were many-headed monsters. Among them was a grandmother giant with 900 heads.

Another giant in nonhuman form was the mighty Thunderbird, described in the tribal legends of various North American Indians. When the Thunderbird flapped its wings, thunder was heard; and when it opened and closed its eyes, lightning arced across the sky.

GNOME

Deep under the ground live the gnomes, a race of dwarflike beings who guard treasures, mines, and quarries. The famous Swiss-German physician Paracelsus, who lived from 1493 to 1541, believed that gnomes could move through solid earth as easily as fish swim through water.

GOBLIN

Like brownies, whom they often resemble, house goblins are little people who help with chores around the house. Other types of goblins, however, are fierce and evil creatures who are enemies of mankind.

House goblins — helpful though they are — tend to be nuisances. Imagine being asleep at night when suddenly your blanket is snatched away. And that may be only the beginning.

If the house goblin still feels like playing pranks, you may spend the rest of the night awake, listening to the sounds of furniture being moved, dishes being broken, and walls being rapped.

GREMLIN

One of the little people was born in the Air Age — a small, troublesome fellow called the gremlin. His main job is to cause difficulties, like engine trouble, on airplanes, especially those flown by the military. However,

some gremlins have a good heart, too. These have been known to help pilots fly damaged airplanes safely home.

Gremlins achieved their greatest fame during World War II, when military airplanes were in the skies everywhere. "Oddly enough," a wartime article on these imaginary creatures commented, "gremlins have no wings and always fly as passengers."

Perhaps because they lack wings, some gremlins prefer to work on the ground. Or possibly ground gremlins are older air gremlins who have retired from flight duty but still want to keep active. Whatever the case, gremlins are also known to cause trouble on the ground:

If a car runs out of gas, is the driver always to blame for being careless? Could your friend really have avoided sitting on your sandwich? Did the refrigerator stop because the pump is worn and should have been replaced?

Can you be sure that the guitar string broke because the peg was turned too tight? Sensible people would generally answer yes to these questions. But, as you know by now, sensible people cannot see gremlins.

IMP

That small demon known as an imp is the errand boy of the supernatural world. In many superstitious tales, he served the Devil as one of the lesser spirits who mostly followed orders. He carried messages, performed everyday chores, and sometimes acted as the *familiar* of a witch.

If an imp became a familiar, he would assume the form of a small animal, like a cat, in order to pass without suspicion among people. He would advise the witch, act as her companion, and run errands of wicked purpose for her.

The superstitious belief in witchcraft has mostly disappeared. With it has gone much of the evil meaning of *imp.* Today the term is sometimes used to mean one of the little people, say an elf or gremlin. It also describes, often with affection, a mischievous child.

LEPRECHAUN

This Irish elf is a shoemaker by trade and a mischief maker by nature. He looks like an old man, is under 2 feet tall, and dresses in a lace coat, cocked hat, and silver-buckled shoes. And he owns a great hidden treasure.

He can be compelled to reveal the location of his treasure but will instantly vanish if one takes his eyes off him. "Is your cow sick?" the leprechaun will ask the farmer, pretending concern and pointing with a finger. Poor farmer. In the very instant that he shifts his eyes, the leprechaun will be gone, taking with him the farmer's dream of riches.

Even if a leprechaun is kept in sight, he has other tricks to protect his treasure. Irish legend tells of a man who made a leprechaun lead him to his gold. It was near a bush, which the man marked with a red garter.

The man thanked the leprechaun and ran to get a spade. He was back in only 3 minutes, ready to dig. But the leprechaun was gone, and as far as the man could see, every bush in the field had a red garter tied to it.

LITTLE PEOPLE

Those imaginary creatures, the little people, live in many parts of the world. We tend, however, to be most familiar with little people from Europe — elves, leprechauns, gnomes, dwarves, pixies, goblins, and the like. But if a United Nations of Little People is ever formed, many other little people are sure to become better known.

From the African country of Dahomey, for example, will come the *aziza,* with their powerful magic. Brazil and Trinidad will send the gay and childlike *ere.* Great numbers of little people from North American Indian tribes will certainly join.

The *wanagemeswak,* who are the little people of the Penobscot Indians, of Maine, are especially worth meeting. However, you can only see them from the side. They are so thin that they are invisible when viewed from the front — unless, perhaps, you are cross-eyed.

MERMAID

The green-black night is calm. A thin track of moonlight on the water points to a scattering of rocks in the shallows. The moonlight flows up from the water onto a flat rock and glows on a being that is part woman.

In place of legs, she has a graceful, scaly tail, like that of a large fish. But from the waist up, she has the body and head of a woman. Her long hair, which she is combing, falls past her shoulders and is either green or gold in color.

This picture of a mermaid is carried in the legends of many countries in the world. Some of the legends say that it is dangerous for sailors to hear a mermaid sing. Her song is very beautiful and the sailors will be attracted to it, wrecking their ship on the rocks where the mermaid lies. Or her song may grow into a wild storm that sinks the ship.

In *A Midsummer Night's Dream,* Shakespeare felt that the magic in a mermaid's singing was so great

> *That the rude sea grew civil at her song,*
> *And certain stars shot madly*
> *from their spheres,*
> *To hear the sea-maid's music.*

MERMAN

Although mermen are not as well known to us as mermaids, they exist in many legends. Mermen vary in their attitudes toward people. Some are helpful, but others bring misfortune.

Abdullah, a poor fisherman in the *Arabian Nights* was helped by a merman who was also named Abdullah. In ancient Babylonia, the merman Oannes taught the people how to build houses, how to plant crops, and how to write.

The handsome, bearded mermen of Danish stories are also friendly beings. But the mermen of Germany and Iceland are dangerous and are to be avoided. So are the mermen of China who are said to be so strong that they can turn over entire ships.

A long time ago, according to a merman legend, a tribe of people lived in a far western land that was cold and had little food. A merman rose from the sea one day and came to them near the shore.

He had green hair and a green beard with a body that was human from the waist up. Instead of legs, he had 2 fishtails. The features of his face were part human and part porpoise.

The merman told the people that he could lead them east across the sea to a milder land. There they would find more food and a better climate. Since the people were starving, they decided to build boats and follow the merman.

The unusual water caravan got under way. The merman swam ahead, singing to the people, encouraging them, and acting as their guide. After they reached the new land, the people watched the merman swim far out into the deep sea, where he disappeared forever. This, the legend tells us, is how the Indians came to North America from Asia.

OGRE

What fear and wonder and imagination have gone into inventing the creatures we call ogres! Monsters all, they are hideous in appearance, often eat people, and usually are quite stupid. They live in the dark and distant places of the supernatural world. When they come out to do battle, they are full of power and fury — but almost always can be outwitted by a clever hero.

Ogres vary greatly in size and shape. They appear as giants, animals, creatures with both human and animal features — and mixtures of these types. In Scotland and Ireland, the ogre is commonly a giant. He is a 7-headed snake in Hungary, a dragon in Greece, and a giant bird called Big Owl in the land of the Apache Indians.

Ogres that are part land animal and part water animal exist in legends throughout the world, for example, in the Far East, in Scandinavian countries, and in the Mayan and Aztec civilizations.

The dragons of Europe are enormous firebreathing ogres with bodies resembling winged lizards. They are terrifying enemies of humanity. You would probably not care to meet one, unless you are out to become a hero or want to steal his fortune — dragons always guard great hidden wealth.

If you meet a dragon in China, however, you have reason to rejoice. Chinese dragons, though sometimes fierce, are not ogres. In fact, the opposite is true — they are kindly and generous creatures. Many legends tell of gifts of wisdom, wealth, and magic that they have given to strangers.

PIXY (OR PIXIE)

Go to Cornwall and Devonshire, in southwest England, and you will hear superstitious people say that pixies dance by moonlight to the music of crickets and frogs.

Pixies are handsome elf-like creatures who dress in green. They are the chief pranksters of the little people who live in the woods. Their victims are mostly unsuspecting people, especially travelers who can be led astray.

Before a pixy completes a night's work, he may misdirect a stranger down a road that ends in a far-off meadow, bang on the walls of a house to frighten the people inside, surprise a girl with a kiss, and take a horse out for a ride. Only then, perhaps, will he return to the rock that serves as his pixyhouse.

If we call somebody a *pixy,* we mean that he is playful and mischievous. But if we call him *pixilated,* it is quite another thing. We regard his behavior as odd, whimsical, even confused — that is, he acts as if he were being led about by a pixy.

POLTERGEIST

Cra-a-sh, R-r-r-ip, Eee-yo-eee. A poltergeist is at work. The word itself tells what is hap-

pening: *poltergeist* means *noisy ghost* in German.

When a poltergeist moves into a house, the people who live there supposedly will be harassed by all kinds of noises and disturbances.

For example, it is claimed that poltergeists rap on walls, move furniture, throw food and dishes around, howl, smash flower pots, ring doorbells, and occasionally burn down houses.

SPIRIT

Any supernatural being, like a ghost or an elf, is generally regarded as a spirit. Those who believe in spirits claim that they are all around us in great numbers. As John Milton, the poet, wrote:

> Millions of spiritual creatures
> walk the earth
> Unseen, both when we wake, and
> when we sleep.

Many different beliefs exist about nonhuman spirits in nature. Some of these grew from the widespread faith that man has an inner force of life — a soul — that is separate from his body.

In beliefs about nonhuman spirits, practically all natural things have spirits, just as men have souls. Some examples are mountains, trees, stones, forests, rivers, diseases, winds, and lightning. Such spirits often have a shape that is human or part human and part animal.

TROLL

Trolls come in 2 sizes. Most are tiny creatures that are really dwarves (and are described under that entry). But in Scandinavian legends, trolls frequently are giants of immense strength and small intelligence. They usually guard treasures that are hidden in the castles in which they live.

VAMPIRE

"Within stood a tall old man . . . clad in black from head to foot, without a single speck of colour about him anywhere. . . . His eyebrows were very massive, almost meeting down over the nose. . . . The mouth was fixed and rather cruel looking, with peculiarly sharp teeth. . . . The Count's eyes gleamed. . . ."

And millions of people shuddered. The vampire Count Dracula has chilled and entertained fans of horror stories since 1897, when he appeared in a novel by Bram Stoker.

The novel and a later play and films did much to popularize vampires — corpses without souls that rise from their graves and suck the blood from living people.

Supposedly, a person bitten by a vampire usually dies soon afterwards and becomes a vampire himself. Another vampire superstition states that if a cat jumps over a corpse before burial, the corpse will turn into a vampire.

Legends about vampires are found around the world, especially in Slavic countries, like Hungary, Russia, Albania, and Poland. One widespread legend is that a vampire can be destroyed if a wooden stake is driven through its heart. If this is done, the vampire will rest in peace and its soul will be saved.

WEREWOLF

In the year 1598, a French judge was examining a prisoner on trial. Among the questions the judge asked, were these:

"When rubbed with this ointment, do you become a wolf?"

"Do your hands and feet become paws of a wolf?"

"Does your head become like that of a wolf — your mouth become larger?"

Today such questions would seem unreal. But they were considered normal in 16th century Europe, when belief in werewolves was widespread. A werewolf was a person who changed into a wolf at will and prowled through the countryside at night, attacking and eating animals and human beings.

Werewolf legends exist on every continent. The word *werewolf* means *man-wolf* in Old English, from *wer* (man) plus *wulf* (wolf). In regions that have few or no wolves, other animals take their place. For example:

Africa has its werelion, werehyena, and werecrocodile; India its weretiger; China its werefox; Greece its wereboar; and South America its werejaguar.

In Europe, a person could become a werewolf by signing a pact with the Devil. Or he could perform a ceremony in the woods that involved smearing himself with an ointment, putting on a wolf hide, and speaking the words of a magic spell. One also could accidentally become a werewolf, for example, by sleeping on open ground on a Friday night under the full moon.

According to European tales, a werewolf had to resume his human form at dawn. To do this, he removed his wolfskin, which he would then hide. A magic link existed between the werewolf and his wolfskin. Thus a cold breeze blowing across the hidden wolfskin would make the werewolf shiver, no matter where he was. And the werewolf would die if somebody destroyed the wolfskin.

ZOMBI

If zombis were for real and you met one walking on a road, it would be a chilling experience. But you would have little to fear because he probably would continue walking without even turning his head to look at you. A zombi, particularly as described on the island of Haiti, is a walking corpse whose soul and mind were stolen by evil magic.

Those who believe in zombis say they are like mindless robots. They only pay attention to the purpose for which they were created — usually to work as slave labor on farms. If a zombi eats salt, one belief goes, he will return permanently to his grave and find peace.

definitions

of terms in Superstition

Words that may be hard to pronounce are spelled phonetically (according to sound). When these words are spoken, a syllable between two slant marks receives greater emphasis. The list below shows how certain letters in the phonetic spelling are correctly pronounced.

a = a in hat	ee = ee in meet
ay = a in day	o = o in lot
uh = a in ago	ew = oo in boot
i = i in pit	oe = o in go
e = e in met	oh = o in sort
eye = ie in pie	ou = ou in out

amulet /am/ yuh lit
An object that is supposed to contain some form of protective magic or be the residence of a friendly spirit. Amulets are similar to charms, talismans, and fetishes.

anthropology an thruh /pol/ uh jee
The science that studies the development of man, his customs, and beliefs.

anxiety ang /zeye/ uh tee
A vague feeling of fear and nervousness. Often an anxious person does not know what is troubling him.

astrology uh /strol/ uh jee
An ancient method, still popular today, of attempting to foretell the future by studying the position of the sun, moon, stars, and planets. Astrology is based on the idea that the heavenly bodies influence the character and future of men and women on earth. See horoscope.

astronomy uh /stron/ uh mee
The science that studies the heavens.

charm
An object (like an amulet) that is supposed to contain some form of protective magic or be the residence of a friendly spirit. Also any action thought to have magic power — for example, crossing one's fingers or reciting the words of a spell.

conscious /kon/ shuhs
Deliberate and intended — for example, a person is aware of his conscious thoughts. Compare with unconscious.

controlled experiment
An experiment that checks the results of another experiment by leaving out a condition that is being tested.

cult
A group of people who share a very strong devotion to an idea, a person, a principle, or a religion.

cycle /seye/ kuhl
A series of events that continue to happen in the same order.

demon /dee/ muhn
An evil spirit, generally considered to be an ally of the Devil.

disaster superstition sew puhr /stish/ uhn
A superstition related to a powerful force in nature — for example, an earthquake or a volcano.

dowsing /douz/ eeng
Searching for an underground substance, usually water, with the aid of a dowsing rod. Most often the rod is a forked branch. Dowsers also try to find petroleum, treasure, minerals, hidden pipes, etc. Other names for water dowsing are *water witching, witching, water divining, water wishing, water smelling,* and *witch wriggling.*

familiar fuh /mil/ yuhr
A demon that supposedly served as companion and adviser to a witch. Familiars were said usually to take the form of small animals — for example, cats, toads, goats, lizards, and birds.

geology jee /ol/ uh jee
The science that studies the history and structure of the earth's crust.

ghost
The spirit of a dead person or a dead animal.

habit
An act repeated so often that it occurs almost automatically — that is, without thought.

hallucination huh lew suh /nay/ shuhn
A vision of things that are not really present. Hallucinations can be caused by a disturbed mental state or by drugs.

heresy /her/ uh see
The holding of religious opinions opposed to those of a recognized church.

horoscope /hohr/ uh skoep
A forecast of the future, made by an astrologer, based on the position of the sun, moon, stars, and planets.

hysteria hi /ster/ ee uh
A confused mental state in which people behave with uncontrolled feelings, especially fear.

jinx jingks
Something or someone that is supposed to bring bad luck. According to this superstition, an object, a place, a person, or even an idea can be jinxed.

magic
In superstition: an attempt to control events by supposedly supernatural means — for example, trying to keep away evil by drawing a magic circle, chanting certain words, or carrying a lucky charm. On the stage: tricks performed by a magician for entertainment.

medium /mee/ dee uhm
A person who claims to link the spirit world with our world by transmitting messages back and forth.

Middle Ages
A period of approximately 1,000 years, from about the 5th to the 15th century.

numerology new muh /rol/ uh jee
The study of how numbers are supposed to influence human life. Some numerologists, for example, assign different numbers to the letters of the alphabet. Then they substitute these numbers for the letters that spell out a person's name. They claim that the final number they arrive at — through various calculations, such as addition — will reveal the person's character and future.

pact
An agreement, often in writing. A witch supposedly made a pact with the Devil.

phobia /foe/ bee uh
An unreasonable and continuing fear of a particular thing or situation. *Phobia* often appears as part of a larger word. For example, *hypnophobia* is abnormal fear of sleep; *acrophobia* is abnormal fear of high places; and *triskaidekaphobia* is abnormal fear of the number 13.

possessed
Taken over and controlled by a spirit. Mediums claim that during a trance their bodies are possessed by a spirit.

prophesy /prof/ uh seye
To predict the future. A *prophecy* is the actual prediction.

pseudoscience /sew/ doe seye uhns
An activity that appears to be scientific but is not.

psychology seye /kol/ uh jee
The science that studies the mind — how people (or animals) think and act.

rationalize   /rash/ uhn uhl eyez
To make up logical sounding but incorrect reasons for something. A person rationalizes to make himself feel comfortable about an error he believed in or a mistake he made.

ritual   /rich/ ew uhl
Series of acts that are part of a ceremony. A ritual is usually part of a formal occasion, such as a wedding or the launching of a ship. But the word can also mean any series of acts that are regularly followed in the same way. Telling a bedtime story to a child can develop into this kind of ritual.

sabbat   /sab/ uht
A great gathering of witches and demons to honor the Devil. Supposedly the sabbat was held at night in some remote place, like a dark forest, mountain top, or cave. It always ended the minute a rooster crowed in the morning.

sign (in astrology)
One of the 12 parts of the zodiac. Each sign has a span of time, about 1 month, associated with it. Astrologers believe that the character and future of a person are influenced by the sign of the zodiac under which he was born.

sorcery   /sohr/ suhr ee
The supposed use of supernatural powers obtained with the help of evil spirits.

supernatural   sew puhr /nach/ uhr uhl
Outside the known laws and forces of nature. *Super* is Latin for *above* or *outside* and appears in many words — for example, superhuman, supersonic, superman.

superstition   sew puhr /stish/ uhn
A belief or practice that does not rely on fact but is based on fear of the unknown or on ignorance — for example, the belief that stepping on a spider will cause rain.

symbol   /sim/ buhl
Something, often a sign, that represents something else — for example, a plus sign, a dollar sign, a cross, and an arrow are all symbols.

sympathetic magic
Control of a person, animal, object, or event by either of 2 principles: 1) Like produces like — for example, a drawing of a deer pierced by arrows supposedly would help a tribe's real hunters repeat the scene. 2) Things that were once in contact always retain a magic connection — for example, a man supposedly could be harmed if a lost tooth fell into enemy hands.

trance
A sleeplike state in which a person is not aware of what is going on around him. People who have been in a trance sometimes believe they have communicated with a dead person or have seen into the future.

unconscious   un /kon/ shuhs
Not deliberate and not intended. Unconscious feelings are ones that a person is not aware of. Compare with conscious.

witch
Originally: a person who engaged in supernatural activities — for example, fortune telling, making magic charms, and controlling future events. In Europe during the 16th and 17th centuries, *witch* took on a new meaning: a person who had made a pact (agreement) with the Devil. Thus witches were said to be part of the Devil's plot to overthrow the Christian religion.

witch doctor
Among primitive people, a person with supposedly supernatural powers who performs such acts as healing the sick, making predictions, speaking with spirits, finding the best hunting areas, and causing rain to fall. Other names for a witch doctor are medicine man, shaman, and sorcerer.

zodiac   /zoe/ dee ak
A circular band of the sky divided by astrologers into 12 equal parts, or *signs.*

recommended books

THE DEVIL IN MASSACHUSETTS by Marion L. Starkey. A dramatic and well researched account of the Salem witch trials. Doubleday. Paperback, $1.75.

DIARY OF A WITCH by Sybil Leek. Story of a woman who claims to be a modern witch — fun to read but not to be taken seriously. Signet. Paperback, $.75.

EAST O' THE SUN AND WEST O' THE MOON by George W. Dasent. The people of the 4 winds, wise animals, giant trolls, and many other imaginary creatures are brought to life in these tales from Scandinavia. Dover. Paperback, $3.00.

THE ENCYCLOPEDIA OF WITCHCRAFT AND DEMONOLOGY by Rossell Hope Robbins. The most complete account of the subject available, written by one of the consultants for this book. Crown. Hardcover, $7.50.

ERROR AND ECCENTRICITY IN HUMAN BELIEF by Joseph Jastrow. A psychologist examines some of the strange beliefs that men have held throughout history. Dover. Paperback, $2.00.

ESP, SEERS, AND PHYSICS by Milbourne Christopher. Mediums, water dowsing, astrology, and many superstitious practices are exposed by the famous magician-author. T. Y. Crowell. Hardcover, $6.95.

FADS AND FALLACIES by Martin Gardner. An excellent discussion of many pseudo-scientific beliefs. Dover. Paperback, $2.00.

FAIRY TALES FROM VIET NAM retold by Dorothy Lewis Robertson. Talking animals, magic jewels, and supernatural creatures provide insight into some beliefs of the Vietnamese people. Dodd. Hardcover, $3.50.

FOLK TALES FROM RUSSIAN LANDS translated by Irina Zheleznova. Here you will meet a witch, a 12-headed monster, a magic violin, dragons, and many more supernatural beings. Dover. Paperback, $2.00.

GHOSTS, SPOOKS, AND SPECTRES by Charles Molin. A rich collection of humorous and eerie stories of the supernatural by celebrated authors. D. White. Hardcover, $3.75.

GOD IS A MILLIONAIRE by Richard Mathison. Examines some fradulent religious cults and why people have followed them. Charter (Bobbs). Paperback, $1.75.

HAWAIIAN MYTHS OF EARTH, SEA, AND SKY by Vivian L. Thompson. These stories of the natural phenomena and wonders of the islands were first told by the ancient peoples of Hawaii at gatherings lit by the flickering light of candlenut torches. Holiday House. Hardcover, $4.50.

HOAXES by Curtis D. Macdougall. Discussion of deliberate frauds and why many people fell for them. Dover. Paperback, $2.00.

HOUDINI ON MAGIC edited by Walter B. Gibson and Morris N. Young. The great magician explains how magic tricks are performed and how he exposed many mediums. Dover. Paperback, $1.75.

HOW DID IT BEGIN by R. Brasch. Reveals the origins of common superstitions, customs, and habits. McKay. Hardcover, $5.50.

A MODERN LOOK AT MONSTERS by Daniel Cohen. Explores myths and superstitions about such creatures as the Loch Ness Monster and Abominable Snowman. Dodd. Hardcover, $5.95.

MOUND BUILDERS OF ANCIENT AMERICA: THE ARCHAEOLOGY OF A MYTH by Robert Silverberg. Thorough discussion of how a mythology grew about the Indian mounds of America. New York Graphic Society. Hardcover, $10.00.

MYSTERIOUS PLACES by Daniel Cohen. Superstitions and facts about Atlantis, Stonehenge, Camelot, etc. Dodd. Hardcover, $5.95.

116

MYTHS OF THE HINDUS AND BUDDHISTS by Aanada Coomaraswamy and Sister Nivedita. Stories taken from the great treasure of Indian mythology. Dover. Paperback, $3.00.

MYTHS OF THE SPACE AGE by Daniel Cohen. Discusses flying saucers, astrology, and other pseudoscientific beliefs. Dodd. Hardcover, $5.95.

NINE TALES OF COYOTE by Fran Martin. Legends of the animal god Coyote, mostly from stories told by the Nez Perce Indians. Harper & Row. Hardcover, $3.25.

OCCULT AND SUPERNATURAL PHENOMENA by D. H. Rawcliffe. A psychological exploration of ghosts, automatic writing, mind reading, and similar subjects. Dover. Paperback, $3.50.

OLODE THE HUNTER AND OTHER TALES FROM NIGERIA by Harold Coulander and Ezekiel Eshugbayi. Traditional tales from Africa that explain natural phenomena and the ways of beasts and men. Harcourt. Hardcover, $3.75.

OZARK MAGIC AND FOLKLORE by Vance Randolph. Legends, beliefs, and odd customs of the hill people of Missouri and Arkansas. Dover. Paperback, $2.50.

PANORAMA OF MAGIC by Milbourne Christopher. Beautifully illustrated history of stage magic and the men who make a profession of fooling people. Peter Smith. Hardcover, $5.00. Dover. Paperback, $2.75.

PINK FAIRY BOOK by Andrew Lang. Supernatural creatures inhabit these legends from many parts of the world, including Africa, Japan, Italy, and Scandinavia. Dover. Paperback, $1.95.

THE RED KING AND THE WITCH by Ruth Manning-Sanders. One of the few collections of gypsy stories of the supernatural. Roy. Hardcover, $4.75.

THE SEA OF GOLD AND OTHER TALES FROM JAPAN adapted by Yoshiko Uchida. Graceful tales of colorful creatures, such as a long-nosed goblin, a shrewd monkey, and a formidable river ogre. Scribner. Hardcover, $3.95.

SECRET SOCIETIES edited by Norman MacKenzie. History of the rituals and beliefs of secret societies — excellent illustrations. Holt. Hardcover, $9.95.

SPIRITS, STARS AND SPELLS by L. Sprague and Catherine de Camp. Entertaining and informative account of strange beliefs. Canaveral Press. Hardcover, $5.95.

THE SUPERNATURAL by Douglas Hill and Pat Williams. A well illustrated introduction to many superstitious practices and beliefs. Hawthorn. Hardcover, $12.95. Signet. Paperback, $.95.

TALES FROM A FINNISH TUPA by James Cloyd Bowman and Margery Bianco. Ancient myths, legends, and animal tales passed on through generations of Finnish storytellers. A. Whitman. Hardcover, $3.50.

13 GHOSTS by Dorothy Gladys Spicer. A phantom ship, a supernatural spider, and a fearsome ghost are some of the mysterious creatures that haunt these stories. Coward. Hardcover, $3.64. Other "13 books" by the author include stories about devils, giants, goblins, monsters, and witches.

WELSH LEGENDARY TALES by Elisabeth Sheppard-Jones. Stories from Wales filled with fairies, elves, magic, and enchantment. Nelson. Hardcover, $3.50.

WHEN THE STONES WERE SOFT by Eleanor B. Heady. How-and-why legends about the beginning of things in East Africa. Funk & Wagnalls. Hardcover, $3.50.

WHICH WAS WITCH? by Eleanore J. Jewett. Tales of ghosts and magic from Korea, told with delicate spookiness and good humor. Viking. Hardcover, $3.50.

index

acknowledgments

We are grateful to the following organizations and individuals for the photographs, art, and information they contributed to this book. Credits are listed by page numbers and letters (T for top, B for bottom, L for left, R for right, and C for center).

Aesop's Fables, translated by Denison B Hull, copyright 1960, U of Chicago Press 99B
Associated Research, Inc 86
Association for Research and Enlightenment, Inc 94T
Bodleian Library 8B
British Museum 37BL
Buffalo Museum of Science 41
Burton, Harry (Metropolitan Museum of Art) 44
Cartier, Inc 15T
Chinese Information Service 48
Cooper-Hewitt Museum (Smithsonian) 14
Cornell University Library 71B
The East Publications, Inc 28
Essex Institute, Salem, Mass 77B
French Government Tourist Office 33T
Garrison, Ron (San Diego Zoo) 22
Geological Survey (USDI) 98B
German Information Center 31 both
Goldman, Luther C (Sport Fisheries and Wildlife — USDI) 43
Jackson, H (Sport Fisheries and Wildlife — USDI) 42B
Library of Congress 63, 93
Lick Observatory 38B, 39, back endpaper
Lieberman, Nathaniel 6B, 7 both, 19, 20, 23B, 32, 54, 58B, 84 both, 85, 88, 89, 99T, 102
Maura, Frederic (Bahama News Bureau) 96
Melander, L M (Library of Congress) 21
Metropolitan Museum of Art, Gift of Henry Walters, 1915 9R
Metropolitan Museum of Art, Rogers Fund, 1934 9L
Minnesota Twins 64
Moreton, Ann 59
Mott, Jacolyn A cover art, 46, 47T, 51, 55, 67, 68, 72, 74 both, 87T, 99B, 103
Mount Wilson and Palomar Observatories 100T
Museum of the American Indian, Heye Foundation 35B
National Gallery of Art 37T
National Water Well Assoc 80
Newkirk, Gordon (High Altitude Obs — NCAR) 61
NY Public Library (Picture Collection) 8T, 10, 12 both, 13T, 16T, 27, 36, 37BR
Oldenkamp, John (Psychology Today) front endpaper, 79
Charles E. Peterson 60B, 95
Richie, Robert (Gulf Oil Corp) 81
Roberts, H. Armstrong 4
Roth Agency 6T, 16B, 38T, 40T, 78B, 83, 94B, 101T
San Diego Zoo 24
Savoy Hotel of London 5
Sexton, Markham W 77T
Shearer, A (NFB of Canada) 34, 35T
Spanish Tourist Office (Museo Lazaro Galdeano) 73
Swedish Information Service 29
Time Pattern Research Institute 15B
Unesco Courier 47B
United Feature Syndicate, Inc, copyright 1959 (Linus said that Miss Othmar . . .) 25
United Feature Syndicate, Inc, copyright 1959 (. . . and then on Halloween . . .) 101B
United Nations 13B, 62, 90
United Press International 58T, 100B
US Bureau of the Mint 40B
USDA 42T
US Defense Dept (Marine Corps) 87B
USDI (Indian Arts and Crafts Board) 26
US Treasury Dept 60T
Universal Pictures 18
Walt Disney Productions 57